2—

COMPLETE GUIDE TO
WALLEYE FISHING

By ART MORASKI

COMPLETE GUIDE TO
WALLEYE FISHING

By ART MORASKI

Illustrations by SCOTT ZOELLICK

Printed in the U.S.A.

ISBN 0-932558-12-7

PHOTO CREDITS: Dave Csanda; Dan Sura; The In'fisherman,
Mid West Outdoors; Captain Bart Blaha; Captain Wayne Orris
and Carl Baker.

This book is dedicated to my wife, Kathy, and children, Art Jr., Nancy Marie, Adalbert and Curt Scott.

ABOUT THE AUTHOR

Art Moraski makes his home in Delafield, Wisconsin. He is a skilled fishing technician and exhaustive researcher specializing, of course, in walleyes. The recognized master on walleye behavior, Art researched the night movements of fish for over seven years, detailing this aspect of the fisherman's world in the classes he taught at Al Lindner's In' Fisherman Schools for several years.

In June of 1978, Art reaffirmed his reputation as a walleye master by winning the National Walleye Tournament. Art became Champion among 200 other competitors in a contest plagued by high winds and rough water. Under these extremely difficult conditions, Art consistently found walleyes when others could not. During an interview following the tournament, Art aptly credited his success to intimate knowledge of walleye behavior and the ability to adapt to prevailing conditions.

Other books by Art Moraski include: Night Fishing I; Night Fishing II; The Sucker Method; The Consumer Guide Of Fishing 1977; The Consumer Guide of Fishing 1978; The Whole Fishing Catalog.

Magaizine credits include: *Fishing Facts; Wisconsin Sportsman; In'Fisherman; Minnesota Sportsman; The Rapala Fishing Guide.*

CONTENTS

AUTHOR'S INTRODUCTION

If I were asked to describe my impression of the walleye, I believe the phrase, "mystical big-eyed wonder with a disposition of a mule" would be more than fitting. When cooperative, the walleye is the easiest fish to catch of all. However, when they're in a neutral to negative mood (which is the case most of the time) you can hardly entice them with offerings that would compare to a steak and lobster dinner to us.

Catching walleye on a consistent basis requires three important elements: (1) fish; (2) adequate equipment and (3) practice on the water. The latter element in time evolves into walleye "savvy". All three of these ingredients must join together to form a successful fisherman. Intelligent fishing is a must, but it's easy to learn how.

This text is a tool, a valuable tool that allows minds-eye participation in the game plan of catching walleye. It is the most complete walleye fishing guide ever assembled. The information is valid and can be applied to any body of water in the world that contains walleye. Read on and study this text with expectations of catching walleyes.

SECTION I

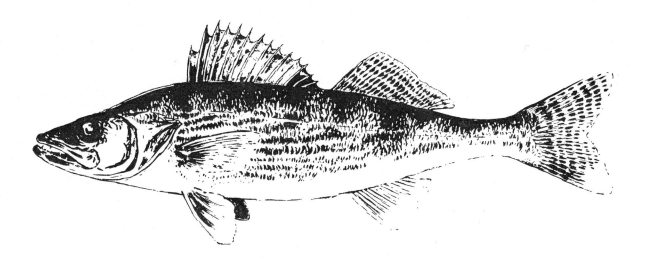

DESCRIPTION

Walleye *(Stizostedion vitreum, Mitchill)*
Walleyes are members of the perch family. Its body is slender, long and designed by nature to over-come its prey with short bursts of speed. It cannot turn on a dime like a largemouth bass nor give a long chase such as the northern pike or muskie. The body has sand-paper like scales of a quarter inch or less in small to medium size fish. The first dorsal fin is supported by strong, sharp spiny rays. The second dorsal and anal fins are soft and the tail is moderately forked.

Being a predator, the mouth is large and lined with canine teeth. The head is slender and gills are covered by firm, sharp subopercle and opercle bones that can easily cut a careless handler. The walleyes eyes are a dead give-away. They are large and opaque. The walleye can see exceptionally well after dark or in turbid water. Their eyes are reflective and glow like a cats eyes when spotlighted at night.

The color of the walleye is regulated by the environment in which it resides. A weed orientated walleye is usually very dark, perhaps black with a yellow or dark white belly. In deep water the fish is very light, taking on a light gray, or brassy olive color back and usually pure white belly.

In larger walleye, the back appears to be humped just behind the head. The general appearance of the walleye lays credence to its ability to hunt effectively. Its main diet usually consists of the abundant specie of baitfish that lives in its environment. When hatched, the walleye feeds on plankton, crustaceans, then insect larve. At about three inches in length, it starts to feed on fish. The plankton feeding stops when the walleye reaches approximately six inches. From then on, the principle food becomes fish, larger aquatic insects and occasionally other creatures. In lakes like Winnebago, in Wisconsin; Lake Erie bordered by Michigan, Ohio, Pennsylvania, New York, and Canada; and Mille Lacs in Minnesota, aquatic insects play an important role as a food base for all sizes of walleye. However there is substantial feeding on perch, gizzard shad, alewife, smelt, white bass, sheepshead, and spottail shiners. It is an interesting example of a large lake that has the characteristics of many individual lakes. Almost every lake type can be related to a portion of Lake Erie.

DISTRIBUTION

Each year the walleye is introduced into new bodies of water. Originally, the boundaries of the distribution of the walleye in North America were Great Slave Lake in the northwest and Labrador in the northeast, south to northern Alabama, through Arkansas and west into Nebraska. The largest walleye are coming (1980) from reservoirs and river systems located throughout the south-mid section of the country. Recently a twenty pound, six ounce walleye had been caught in Greer's Ferry Reservoir in Arkansas. Many fish over twelve pounds have come from this reservoir. Others that have big fish potential include; Dale Hollow, Center Hill and Norris in Tennessee; Cumberland in Kentucky; Bull Shoals and Norfork in Arkansas; and Stockton and Table Rock in Missouri.

At this writing, there are three bodies of water in the country that are really hot. They are producing so many walleye that the percentage of productivity per-man-hour staggers the mind.

Mille Lacs Lake in Minnesota; a typical half day stringer will consist of a few two pound fish, a couple between three and five pounds and possibly a six or seven pounder.

Lake Winnebago in Wisconsin; a typical half day stringer will consist of five fish between one and a half to two and a half pounds.

Lake Erie in the east. The best area is in the western basin bordered by Michigan, Ohio and Canada. A typical two hour stringer will consist of a few fish of two pounds or better, a few in the five pound range and some around six or seven pounds. While interviewing Capt. Wayne Orris, he had indicated that on one Friday afternoon, the charter left at 4:30 P. M. and returned at 7:30 P.M. with thirty people aboard. During the three hour period they had caught their legal limit of 320 walleyes ranging from 1-1/2 pounds to 4 pounds (recently the legal limit has dropped from ten fish per person to six fish per person). The extra twenty walleyes belonged to the two man crew. Checking with fisheries biologist Carl Baker and Charter Boat Association President Capt. Bart Blaha, this kind of fishing action is not unusual. Lake Erie is presently the most productive walleye lake in the world. This could change, but for now, recent year classes have spawned successfully and are abundant.

NATURAL DISTRIBUTION of walleyes sauger and blue pike. The walleye has been widely stocked in recent years outside its original range.

Map courtesy Great Lakes Fishery Commission

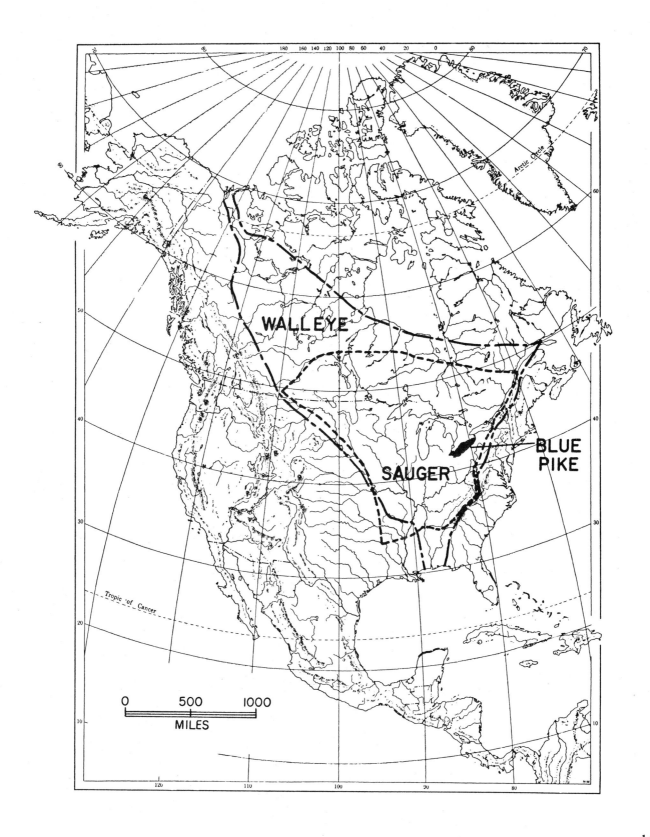

SECTION II

FISHING THE LAKES: SEASON-TO-SEASON

A1   LAKES DURING SPRING; Pre-spawn
The big move

The spawning movement is on as soon as water temperatures change slightly from the ice cold low thirties to the high thirties. The change of water temperature is a stimulant, induced by nature to trigger the spawn instinct of the species. The entire biological clock is regulated by temperature change. As if signaled by a starting gun, the walleye makes its big move toward adequate spawning areas.

The males are first to arrive on the scene. An army of one to three pound fish infiltrate the shallows. The wind-swept shores, generally the northeast and northwest shorelines of the lake (if accompanied by the right type of bottom) are the first to receive spawning action because usually they are the first shorelines to warm up. With water temperatures in the high thirties, small groups of males gather near spawning areas. As the temperatures increase to the low forties, larger groups congregate. The optimum temperature for penetration of the males is about forty-four degrees.

Lake water is usually quite clear after the settling of dirt particles from ice-out. Because of this, movement into the shallows by males usually takes place at night. If you stand on the shoreline and point a flashlight into the water, and you are in the proper area, you should see many walleyes moving about. It will look like an expressway interchange with headlights moving in all directions. The walleyes eyes reflect the light from your flashlight. They will spook briefly and return to the same area soon after the light is turned off. During the daylight hours, the males back off into deeper water or sheltered areas in proximity to the main spawning site. The depth is usually indicated by point of visibility; meaning just beyond the point where you lose contact with the bottom visually. In some lakes that daytime holding depth may be twenty feet deep while in murky waters it may be five feet deep. The holding depth will also be dependent upon the bottom content. If the bottom is quite weedy, the males will use the weeds for cover. Whatever the case, the males are in large schools and vulnerable to the lures and baits to be discussed later.

A2   All of the males are not collectively grouped at prime spawning areas during the same time. A majority of males are in prime spawning areas, others have not received natures message yet. Often they live in portions of the lake that have not yet warmed. This may be nature's way of protecting the species.

Let's take the example of a lake that is five miles long, running north to south. The north end will warm up quicker, receiving more sunlight during the day. The southern end may be as much as five to ten degrees cooler. Resident fish from the north end may be in full spawning posture while the southern end has yet to receive schools of males. The deeper the lake the greater the possibilities of this happening. The end result is the possibility of finding groups of males on one side of the lake; fishing for them until spawning actually occurs; then moving to another area and catching them in the beginning of their spawning run.

A3   LAKES DURING SPRING; Pre-spawn
Locating large females

That potential trophy fish, the female, is full of spawn, weighing as much as it will ever weigh during the season at hand. Dreams of that ten pound fish lie hidden in every fisherman's mind.

Some states have a closed season for walleyes. That makes it difficult to fish for some of those pre-spawn females. However, some lakes may be open to fishing. Occasionally, the cold weather lasts for a longer period of time than normal and spawning activity starts near the opening of the season. It appears that the closer it gets to spawning time, the greater number of females group together. During this time of the year, it is the walleyes nature to follow contours; moving along dropoffs, obstructions and concrete walls. Holding areas include: rocky points, saddles, inside and outside turns of the contour, steep cliffs and the like.

In developing a game plan for locating large females, first look for prime spawning areas. Resident females will eventually come to spawn. After finding the spawning bay or shoreline, motor out to the first major drop-off *(See Illustration 101)*. The best spawning area is bay (A1.). Motor out to (D1.) and follow the contour towards (D) and around point (A); then go back and follow it towards (C) and around (B). Now you've located two good starting points, (A) and (B). Chances are one of these two points may hold some of those larger fish. Systematically work around both points slowly, there are no guarantees, but you are sticking to a game plan. It is reasonable to assume that some fish are present . . . be confident of it. If it is early pre-spawn, the points should be good; if it is late pre-spawn the area denoted by (D1) should hold fish.

Points are natural magnets, drawing walleye when food is abundant. Included in the game plan, points (A), (B), (E), and (J) should be worked thoroughly. Spend enough time on each to locate active fish, but don't over do it . . . time is valuable.

The area between point (E) and rock bar (F) is called a "saddle". Some saddles turn out to be year around hot-spots. Particular attention should be given to all saddles. The rock bar (F) has a long side (I), which is on the south side, it will probably warm up sooner than the north side of it. By the same token, (D1), (G1), (E1) and (I) may receive warmer water temperatures first, making them ideal places to search for pre-spawners. The south end of the lake may have delayed spawning activity for another week or two.

Have confidence in yourself, the fish are there. Usually they don't come quick or easy. The large female groups may consist of less than twenty fish (it's more like five or six fish) and each group may occupy less than twenty-five square feet of room when schooled tightly. This means that you could easily skim over a group without actual contact with them.

A4 LAKES DURING SPRING; Pre-Spawn
Choosing the right lures

Many of the lures mentioned in this section can also be used during other times of the year as well. As a result some will be repeated again throughout this book. It is important to realize that each lure is versatile and can be used in many different situations. Fishing for pre-spawn walleyes calls for *slow retrieves,* a *slow troll* and extra care in handling bait. The environment is at a slow pace. The wall-

eye's metabolism is low because of cold water temperatures. When water temperatures reach about sixty degrees, the walleye is at it's optimum feeding temperature and will chase down lures. For now slow methods of presentation is the rule.

In choosing the correct lures for pre-spawn fishing, remember the environment is filled with newly hatched small fish. Some of the baitfish spawn in fall and have not yet grown very large. A small bait is natural in the walleye's environment at this time.

SHALLOW WATER

Time of day, weather conditions and wave action will help to determine the productive depth. The elements will affect your choice of lures. Floating or top water lures are not effective when it's windy with pounding waves rolling up on shore; they are when it's calm and humid. Top water lures can be most effective when they are worked in ten feet of water or less. A stop and go retrieve is a good one to start with. Later as you get the feel for them, you might cast the lure, let it sit on the water, twitch it; retrieve it for a foot or two, then twitch it again. This type of action simulates a wounded minnow. Some of the popular floater imitation minnow types include: Rapala, Cotton Cordell's Red-Fin, Bagley and Rebel. When a slow, straight retrieve is applied, most of these lures will dive and run at about one to three feet below the surface. Some will dive much deeper if the retrieve is faster.

Another tool used in water that is one to ten feet deep, is the "jig and minnow". The jig is one of the most versatile tools used in fishing. Ranging in size from a 1/64 ounce and less to better than a pound (used in saltwater fishing), the jig can be "still fished"; brought in by a straight retrieve; bounced on the bottom or trolled. Some manufacturers feel that the jig looks like a minnow. Whatever the case . . . it is worth while to have a bunch.

A jig can be used with a minnow, nightcrawler, wax worm, leech, etc. Some fishermen use them without any added frills or tasty delights. There are jigs of all types: with bucktail, bear hair, maribou, extra hooks, plastic bodies and on and on. Before getting confused, just start with the basic jig with some type of hair on it. Color is discussed

ILLUSTRATION 101

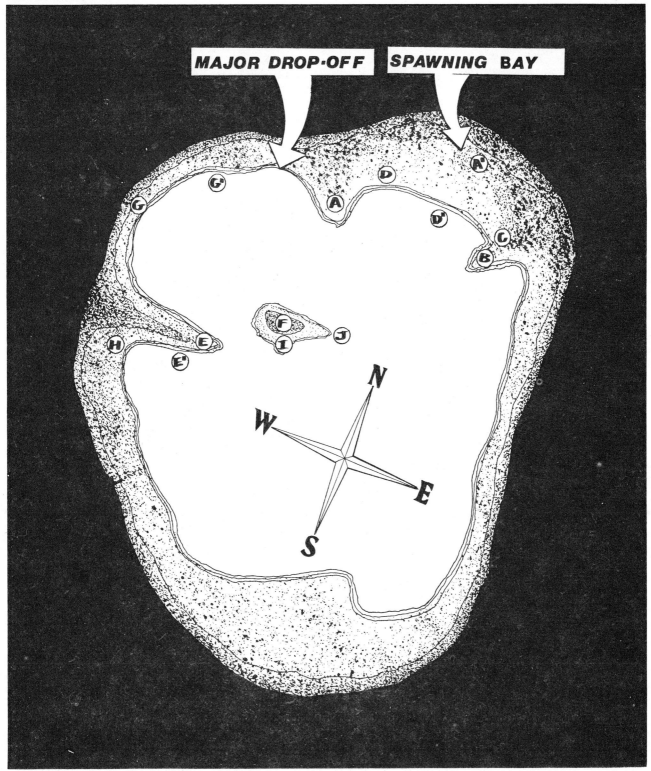

later.

While fishing shallow water, use a 1/4 ounce jig or less. The action is better than heavier ones and it will be less likely to get hung up on every little stone. Their water weight is less, making them appear a bit more natural. Remember, the environment has an abundance of small fish in it. It is natural to have a minnow attached to the jig. The minnow should be between one and three inches long. Hook the minnow upwards, starting from under the mouth, straight through and out the top of the head, making sure the barb of the hook is clear of the head.

One of the problems that a fisherman experiences with a jig and minnow is the loss of minnows during the cast. One jig manufacturer, Grassl's Double OO, offers a jig with a double hook set-up; one held on by a neoprene appendage. This works very well. Another way to over-come the problem (although not completely) is to punch a hole in a piece of plastic (like a coffee can top) with a paper punch. The round piece of plastic should measure approximately 1/4 inch in diameter or less. Secure this piece over the hook after the minnow has been attached. Make sure the plastic goes beyond the barb. This little trick will cut down on the minnow loss due to casting.

Cast the jig and minnow and let it settle to the bottom. Hold your rod at about a three o'clock position. Let it rest on the bottom for about five seconds; lift your rod (moderately) to twelve o'clock; let the jig settle and take up your slack line, again holding at three o'clock. In most cases the walleye will strike while the jig is falling or at a complete stop. You must be prepared for it. . . setting the hook hard and fast. There's no bargaining for a second chance. Besides it doesn't cost a thing to set the hook. So if something feels unusual, set the hook.

There are more types of jigs available to the angler than any other type of lure on the market. Their origins range from small basement operations to mass merchandise manufacturers whose names carry weight in the fishing world. Some of the small operations produce excellent jigs, most of the large jig manufacturers started out small. The best advice I can give on jigs is to check with your local sporting goods store and find out what's selling. Look at all of the jig cards. The ones that are almost gone might be the hot lure in your area.

A bobber, small split shot and minnow combination may not be the most exciting way to fish, but it is certainly effective. It's ironic that most fishermen start out with it and as time goes on, forget its

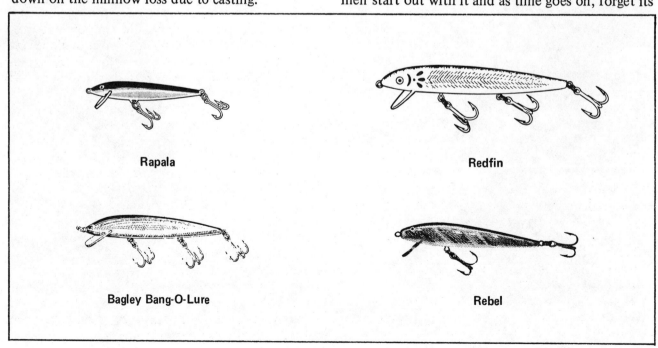

Rapala

Redfin

Bagley Bang-O-Lure

Rebel

JIGGING FOR WALLEYES is one of the top methods used for consistent catches.

value. There are probably more bobbers left in a fisherman's basement than are in tackle boxes. The bobber allows you to change depth instantly. The change may be the difference between a stringer of fish or none at all.

Imagine yourself as a sluggish old walleye, lying on the bottom, not really hungry; unless something came by that was so easy, you could hardly resist. While tending to your own business, gazing at nothing in particular; a splash occurs just above you. In sheer desperation, not knowing whether to dart off and hide or just stay put; you choose the latter. Almost instantly, a minnow desends, perched just above your reach. It squirms, and hardly maintains its balance swimming in a circle. Obviously it's different than the rest of the minnows that require much more energy to capture. This one's wounded and if I don't devour it, someone else will!

Obviously the walleye does not go through this thinking process. However, its laws of survival are clear-cut.

One effective method of using this rig in shallow water is to use the bobber and minnow without a sinker when the walleyes are super shallow. Set the bobber approximately two feet above the hook. Hook the minnow at a point just in back of the dorsal fin (the top fin). The fleshy top half of the back is usually hooked, otherwise you may kill the minnow. Cast it toward the shallows (in about three feet of water and less). Retrieve it a foot or two in ten to fifteen second intervals. To work a little deeper, slide the bobber up another foot or two and attach a split shot sinker mid-way between the bobber and hook. Repeat the retrieve procedure.

MEDIUM DEPTH OF WATER

To put this into perspective, I call medium depth eight to fifteen feet deep. There's a regiment of lures that fall into this catagory. I'll explain the basics and you can take it from there.

23

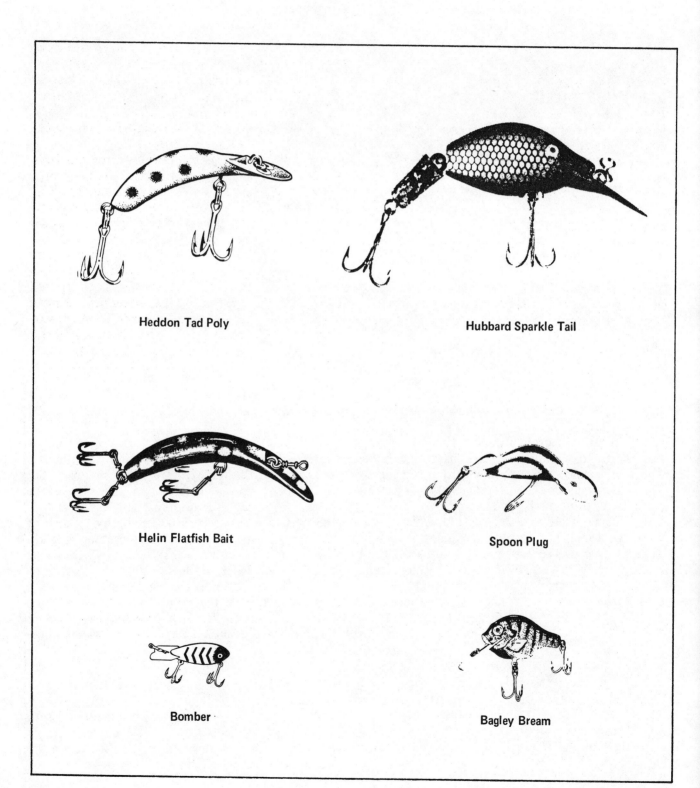

Heddon Tad Poly

Hubbard Sparkle Tail

Helin Flatfish Bait

Spoon Plug

Bomber

Bagley Bream

Crankbaits fit into this catagory. "Crankbait" is just a name given to an assortment of lures that dive upon retrieve or "cranking". A common characteristic is a plastic or metal lip causing the bait to dive. Often they look like a baitfish of sorts. Usually the depth by which it will hold upon a steady retrieve is determined by the size and shape of the lip. Other factors such as diameter of line; stretch of line and wire line will also effect the lures depth of travel. Large diameter line tends to make a lure ride higher in the water; small diameter lines will have less water resistance, allowing the lure to travel at its prescribed depth. Wire line has the ability to cut water and by its weight allows the lure to travel deeper, quicker. The speed of retrieve makes a difference also. The slower the retrieve, the higher the lure will ride in the water.

There are several methods of retrieve that can be used with crank-baits. The simplest, is casting the lure and retrieving it slowly. Pre-spawn calls for slower retrieves than one might be accustomed to.

Another effective method is to cast the lure and start a lightening fast retrieve as soon as it hits the water. Do this for a few seconds so the lure can get down to its prescribed depth, then resume your slow retrieve.

The stop-and-go retrieve will work better as water temperatures warm up. Cast out the lure, start your retrieve and continue it for approximately ten feet; stop for a split second, then resume. Continue this all the way back to the boat. At times a walleye will give chase. The split second stop forces the fish to make a quick decision . . . strike or pass it up!

There are two basic crank-bait classifications: tight-action cranks and loose action cranks. Tight-action cranks are crank-baits that wobble or vibrate very quickly; and loose action crank-baits have a wider arc in their wobble. A tight-action crank-bait may wobble two hundred times while traveling two feet forward; a loose action crank-bait may only wobble forty times while traveling the same distances.

In the long run, you will catch a greater number of walleyes by using tight-action crank-baits. The flashing lure and slow speed combination fills-the-bill. Walleyes are not known to chase down lures for long distances. The northern pike, muskie and largemouth bass will chase a lure further than the walleye. Some of the tight-action crank-baits offered on the market are: Heddon's Tadpolly, Sparkle-Tail, Flatfish, Spoonplugs (for this depth), Bombers, some of the Bagleys, etc.

Some of the floating top-water lures can be adapted to act like tight-action crank-baits by placing a split-shot weight ahead of the lure. The Rapala and Red-Fin work very well. The weight forces more action on the lure because it keeps it under water. The Rapala is an excellent walleye lure.

The Lindy Rig is a real classic when it comes to walleye catching ability. The Lindy Rig, introduced by Al and Ron Lindner, has become a standard walleye producer with live-bait fishermen. Simple to use, it has helped more fishermen to catch walleye than any other single advancement of a live bait rig since the invention of the hook. The mech-

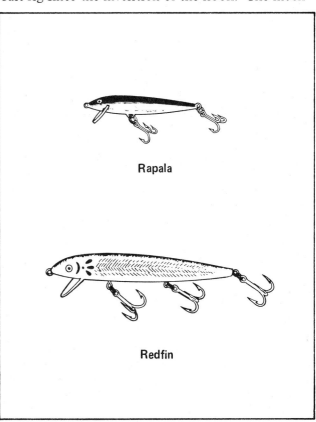

Rapala

Redfin

anics are so simple it's almost absurd. The Lindy Rig consists of: a snell with numbers 4, 6 or 8 hook; a barrel swivel clip; and set of sinkers (some have a 1/8, 1/4, 3/8 or 1/2 ounce weight). The sinkers have a hole in them allowing the free flow of the line. Thread the line from your rod through the sinker and attach the line to the barrel swivel; next slide the loop of the snell over the clip (also on the barrel swivel); hook-up your live bait and you're all set. The principle is easy to understand.

A walleye actively feeds for short periods of time. In most cases you must entice the walleye to strike. A walleye is weight conscious. Often times it will drop your offering at the slightest feel of something unnatural. Here's where the Lindy Rig comes into play. The sinker rests on the bottom, the walleye can pull the line (as you feed it) without feeling weight because the line is passing through the hole in the sinker. The barrel swivel acts as a stopper, this keeps the weight from sliding down to the hook.

The Lindy Rig can be used in almost any depth of water. It can be used with a nightcrawler, leech, leaf worm, salamander, crayfish, etc. It's extremely versatile. It can be "still-fished", trolled, back-trolled or used while drifting. These methods are discussed in other chapters.

The medium depth of water can be covered very well by the jig and minnow as previously mentioned. The Spoonplug deserves added attention. The Spoonplug was developed by Buck Perry. It is available in many sizes, each traveling at its own prescribed depth. A Spoonplug can be speed trolled or just barely crawled along. During this time of the year it is best to just crawl it along. Choose the size that will bump the bottom now and then at the depth you wish to explore. In most instances, the Spoonplug is trolled. Casting it is a bit more difficult.

DEEP WATER

Fifteen feet and deeper is considered deep water to the walleye fisherman. The shallow edge of the deep water can be worked very easily by using the same tools as in the shallow water section. When fishing in twenty, thirty, forty or more feet of

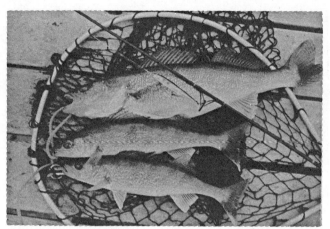

IMITATION MINNOWS are particularly effective during spring and fall.

water, the selection of lures diminishes with depth. Most of the crank-baits are designed to travel at twenty-five feet or less. Deep running crank-baits have large, almost bulky looking lips. They are usually made of thick plastic or metal. Many of the lure bodies are manufactured with materials that are somewhat buoyant, thus a bit more speed is applied to keep them at their prescribed depth. Generally the size of the lure is increased to keep it in balance. So with choosing deep running lures, one must contend with a larger lure (usually) and moderate to fast retrieves or trolling speeds. Some of the better lures on the market are; Bagley, Rebel, Rapala, Spoonplugs, Bomber, Cisco Kid, Creek chub , Pixie, Bill Norman, Mud-Bug, Crankbait Corp., Cordell, and Lindy Shad.

The Lindy-Rig and jig and minnow are excellent tools for working deep water. Usually a 1/2 ounce sinker will do the job, however, if it is windy, a larger weight may be required to stay in contact with the bottom. A jig with a plastic body and swirly tail (Mister Twister Lures) is a good choice. The tail is very tantalizing to walleyes. This combination is best used when the walleye is actively feeding. The cast and retrieve motions are identical to the jig and minnow patterns.

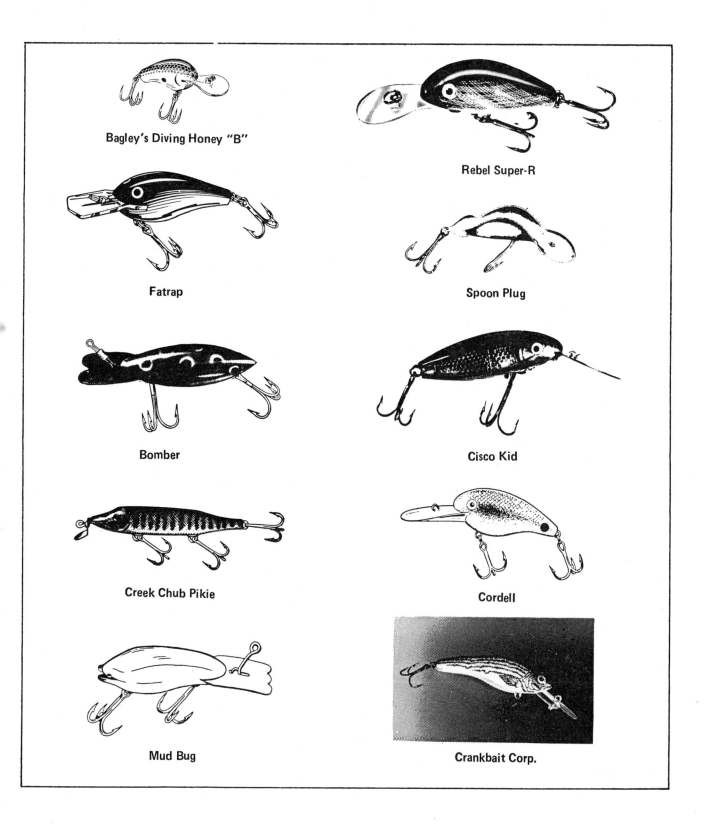

Bagley's Diving Honey "B"

Rebel Super-R

Fatrap

Spoon Plug

Bomber

Cisco Kid

Creek Chub Pikie

Cordell

Mud Bug

Crankbait Corp.

One valuable tool used more in southern waters for walleye than in the north, is the "Spoon". The Spoon I am referring to is a bit different than the common Dardevle, or Little Cleo. These spoons, sometimes referred to as "slab spoons", are usually slender in width; two to five inches in length; have one treble hook attached and weigh between 1/2 and 1 1/2 ounces. The Mann-O-Lure manufactured by Mann's Tackle Company is one of the best, because the spoon is thin enough to bend slightly (with your fingers) making it look like an injured minnow. The Swedish Pimple and Hopkins are also high ranking lures.

The spoons are best used with a straight up and down motion. Your boat control plays an important part in the success you will have with the spoons. The ultimate is to have a boat with an electric trolling motor that can be used for positioning. Position yourself over deep water rock or gravel bars. Plot the bar out closely, so you have a visual concept of its shape. You might be fishing in forty or fifty feet of water! Lower the spoon to the bottom; get a feel for bottom contact. You will get accustomed to knowing the bottom and where the dips and mounds are by feeling it through the spoon.

When the spoon touches bottom, give it a snap with your wrist. The spoon will pop about three feet off the bottom, then with tension (the weight of the spoon descending) on the line, follow your rod back down slowly. The action simulates a dying minnow. As the spoon touches bottom again, repeat the process. Work your way around with the electric motor.

In the case of the Mann-O-Lure, bend the spoon slightly (like the curve of an archers bow). This curve will help in adding action.

The strike is an unusual one. Many times you won't feel anything, but the line will twitch or go slack before the spoon reaches the bottom. DON'T DIP YOUR ROD TO SET THE HOOK. In one motion, set the hook and reel in the line at the same time, all the way up. Hold your rod high. Frequently the strike occurs while the bait is falling. You must practice the method to become effective. And, it only works when the fish are in that depth of water.

Mann's Mann-O-Lure

The average weight of the spoon used in fifty feet of water is one ounce. Adjust according to wind and depth. Try to get away with as light a weight as possible. The angle of descent should be between straight down and about a forty five degree arc. Occasionally an angler will lace a nightcrawler over the treble hook. Sometimes it's needed.

COLOR

Fishermen could argue about colors that work for them for another decade and never really totally agree. Color is a variable that occurs with: depth, water clarity, wind, clouds, the position of the sun, bottom content and available forage fish in the lake.

For example, a particular lake may have had a population of creatures with orange bellies, light green backs and black spots to boot. In that particular lake, lures that are green with black spots may obviously be the hot ones. This is why it is a good idea to check with local fishermen about colors that work at the new lake you plan to fish. Get the basic colors down pat and expand from there.

If you cannot find a reliable source of information then refer to the chart. These colors are basic, the object is to match colors and the environment as closely as possible.

Water Color	Bottom Content	Color of Lure
Clear	Sand	White, Light Brown, Chartreuse, Silver, Black
Clear	Muck	Black, Dark Brown
Clear	Weeds/green	Black, Brown White, Chartreuse, Tan, Gray
Clear	Rocks/Gravel	Black, Brown, Red, Blue, Silver, Orange, White, Purple
Medium or Dark Brown (flowage type water)	Sand/Gravel/ Muck/Weeds	Black, Yellow, Gold, Red, Chartreuse, Orange, Brown, Purple

Waters that are in-between should be judged by their general color. Light color waters, use light color baits; dark water, use dark baits. Minnows tend to take on the natural lights and darks of their environment.

Here's an experiment that will make a believer out of you: say you purchase two dozen large fatheads. Take one dozen and place them in a black bucket; the other in a white bucket. Let them sit for an hour or two. Now take a few of each into a dip net. You will notice that the ones from the black bucket are very dark, while the ones from the white bucket are almost colorless and very light. Minnows that are very close to the surface waters will change shades of color and look a bit darker during long dark cloudy days. By the same token, they will be lighter in color on days of full sunshine.

Referring to the chart, you may wonder why there are so many variations for the "clear water with rocks and gravel" categories. Rocks and gravel draw crayfish, often times they are brown with shades of orange, blue and red. Leeches, another favorite food, are often times black or brown. In addition, black is universal. So, you have a good place to start. You will find your own variations as you progress. Shades of purple and green work well in most waters. If you had to pick three colors that would fit in almost all situations, take black, white and yellow.

LINE

Line is the most important piece of equipment that you use. Often times a fisherman spends forty or seventy dollars on a good rod and reel; a slight fortune on lures, then purchases the cheapest line he can find. It just doesn't make sense. Spend all of that money, spend all of that time in pursuit of his game and then take a chance of losing his quarry due to cheap line.

Line effects the action of a lure, especially when it is tied directly to the lure. There are different grades of line starting with a stiff line and ending with limp line. The degree of stiffness is often dependent upon the diameter of the line. In general terms, a small diameter line is usually soft or limp and wide diameter lines are stiff. A stiff line will restrict the action of certain lures, particularly crank-baits. Their practical use is in trolling, casting spinner baits and with plastic worms or jigs. Lures that impart much of their own action should be fished with small diameter or limp line. Sometimes a compromise is necessary: a ball-bearing snap swivel will help.

Thin diameter lines are needed when fishing under tough conditions, such as a major change in weather (a cold front). When the walleyes are in a negative mood, all the care one can give is necessary; thin diameter line, small baits, and slow fishing methods. If you have to have everything going for you, pay attention to the line size, its neutral color, the size of hook and weight. While fishing slow, the walleye has a chance to observe everything before making a decision. When fishing's easy, you could probably use a kite string and still catch fish. Use line as light as four pound under extreme tough conditions, and ten or twelve

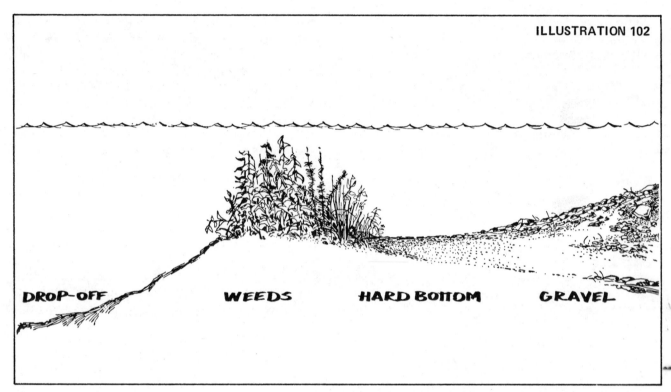

ILLUSTRATION 102

DROP-OFF   WEEDS   HARD BOTTOM   GRAVEL

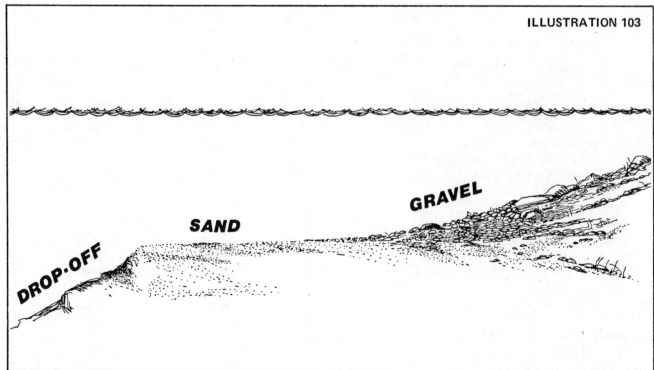

ILLUSTRATION 103

GRAVEL

SAND

DROP-OFF

pound line for trolling. If there are a lot of obstructions you might use a heavier line. As far as color goes, use neutral colors for slow fishing and high visibility lines for fast fishing or trolling.

A major part of the battle of catching walleye is proper bait presentation at the depth most likely to hold fish. Your bait has to be where the fish are. Searching for the proper depth is an important part of your game plan, choosing the correct lure is another.

B1 LAKES DURING SPRING; Spawn
Location Of Spawning Areas

Although spawning areas are typical throughout the United States and Canada, there are slight variations due to the bottom content in lakes and rivers. For instance, a great percentage of river run walleyes in the Fox and Wolf Rivers in Wisconsin spawn in the flooded marshes. Spawning occurs over marsh grass and debris during the high water of spring. This may be an exception to the rule, however, some walleyes have been observed spawning over sandgrass and sand bottom combinations.

Canadian Shield lakes offer a lot of rock, in many cases too much rock, generally in the form of large boulders. The most consistent spawning areas will contain these ingredients: gravel areas stretching outward from shore; gravel shoals; the areas where the gravel and sand meet in relatively shallow water; sand areas that are littered with stones and timber; and near the dams of rivers and creeks.

The upper third of the United States contains more variations of sand, gravel and rocks. In most cases the walleye will choose gravel as prime spawning grounds. Prime spawning areas will have these significant factors: *(Illustration 102)* from shoreward on out: a slight stretch of gravel, hard bottom (possibly sand), then weeds; or *(Illustration 103)* from shoreward out: rock, gravel, then hard bottom associated with a dropoff, all within a short distance from shore.

Sandgrass seems to be an added plus but not a necessary ingredient (sandgrass usually grows on a harder bottom, is brittle and matted). In the case of lakes and flowages that are fed by river systems,

a great portion of the walleye population dwelling near the river system will use the river system as the prime spawning grounds. You may find the use of different spawning times and areas within a large body of water that is fed by a river system.

From the mid-third of the country and south, many river systems are dammed up, creating reservoirs. The head-waters (just below the dams) will receive most of the spawning activity. The hard bottom creek arms that are littered with gravel and timber also play an extremely important role. The best creek arms have definite creek channel dropoffs running into them. Current, whether slight or rushing, is important. The walleyes travel against the current (in most instances) to prime spawn areas and use it to an effortless advantage when returning back to the main body of water.

Spawning usually occurs at night with an optimum water temperature range of forty-eight to fifty-two degrees, but have been known to spawn in cooler and warmer temperature ranges.

With males present, the female makes an appearance on the scene, moving in and out of the choosen area. Occasionally she will rub her belly against the gravel through a series of diving and bumping gestures. The males appear to steer her about until the final states of preparation. When ready, she moves into position and the males (usually one or more on each side) start thrashing against her body depositing fertilization while the eggs drop to the bottom. Often one can hear the splashing on a calm night. The female will for the most part stop feeding during the crucial period.

Exhausted from the strain on her body, she will lazily make her way back toward the safety of deep water. A well placed offering may be consumed, but she's hard to entice during her trip to R & R.

B2 LAKES DURING SPRING; Spawn
Limits Of Milkers

The army of males, or "milkers", are present before, during and after the spawn period. They make their way toward prime spawning grounds in schools and linger there for a long period of time.

As if they were all cut from the same mold, limits of one to three pound fish are common. The males are usually shallow and relatively easy to catch. A known area may produce limits day after day, hardly showing signs of drying up. With the excitement of spawning, their aggressiveness seems to be at its peak.

The magic holding depth during the day-light hours may be approximately fifteen feet or shallower on a body of water that is considered dark to medium clear in coloration. The night-time depth may be eight feet or less on the same body of water. You can adjust accordingly when working clear water during the daytime; however, the night-time depth will still be at an average of eight feet or less. These are approximate depths and will give you a starting point. The prevailing conditions will play an important role in actual location.

The male is a voracious creature often consuming more than it actually needs. While cleaning the catch, it is common to find two or three freshly devoured minnows. In one particular case, I cleaned a small male that had seven small undigested perch in its gullet. This exceptionally positive feeding mood seems to start at their pre-spawn movements, taper off during the actual spawn, then resume during a short post-spawn period.

Minnows represent a major portion of the males diet, with leeches and other aquatic inhabitants second. The ideal size of minnow ranges from 1-1/2 to 3 inches in length and is natural in the walleyes environment. Lake shiners, chubs, golden shiners, river shiners and fatheads represent an excellent selection of baits. In rivers, and flowages: river shiners, golden shiners, fatheads, mud minnows, chubs and willow-cats offer a great variety.

A hook, line and sinker combination is by far the simplest and most widely used rig in live-bait fishing for walleye. As one gets a bit more advanced, the jig and minnow combination and Lindy-Rig offers nearly unlimited potential.

The simple line and sinker set-up should include a number 10 to 12 hook attached to six or eight pound test line; a sinker weighing less than 1/4th ounce when working in shallow water on calm days

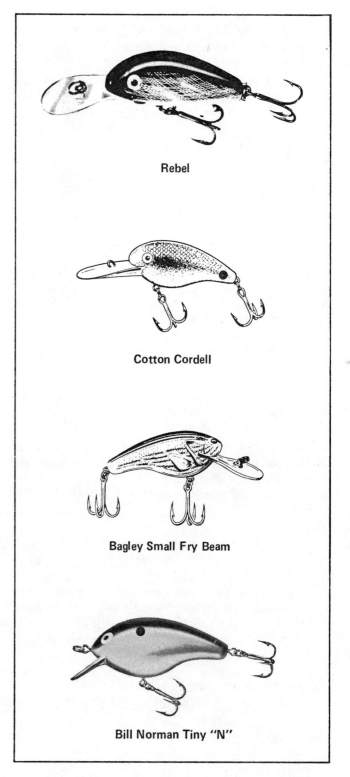

Rebel

Cotton Cordell

Bagley Small Fry Beam

Bill Norman Tiny "N"

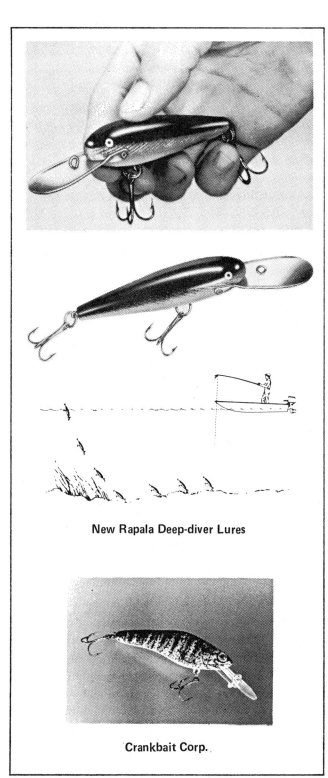

New Rapala Deep-diver Lures

Crankbait Corp.

and a 1/4th ounce *or more* when working a little deeper or during windy days. The distance between sinker and hook is usually more than 12 inches. Ultra-light fishing tackle helps to make catching those males a most enjoyable experience.

Whether you're on shore or in a boat hardly makes a difference in the method of using the simple set-up. Cast to the prospective area, let the rig sink to the bottom, the minnow will do its job. Very slowly, work it back in a stop-and-go type of retrieve. The indication of the strike is usually felt by either two distinct taps or a slight twitch in the line. Sometimes just the feeling of added weight during the retrieve signals "strike". In any case remember, it doesn't cost a penny to set the hook, so set it!

The jig and minnow combination is very popular when fishing for walleyes. It is also effective during the spring of the year. When working in shallow water, a lightly weighted jig seems to work best. They will have a bit of buoyancy and the action of the minnow appears a bit more natural. A round head jig defies water dynamics and has a tendency to roll and pitch giving the minnow added action. It is best used when swimming the jig along the bottom.

If you enjoy using artificial lures, the Rapala is undoubtedly the top-of-the-line. Try the silver and black, or silver and blue combination in clear waters; the gold and black, and flourscent orange and silver combination in darker waters. The Countdown Rapala can be used in fifteen feet of water or less; the Floating Rapala when in shallow or obstruction infested waters.

Retrieves can vary. They include: slowly twitch the Rapala all the way back to the boat (or shore); or retrieving as fast as you can, with a split second stop occasionally; or use a straight retrieve, giving the lure a jerk every so often.

Other manufacturers having similiar lures are: Rebel, Cotton Cordell, The Crankbait Corporation, Bagley and Bill Norman lures. Each area will have its own particular favorite.

Spend most of your time, near prime spawning areas and the routes that lead to these areas. Many fishermen fish at the head-waters of a river system and forget holding areas en route to the head-waters that are virtually un-touched. Take some time, research the area. You might find a honey-hole.

B3   LAKES DURING SPRING; Spawn
The uncooperative female

The female *can* be caught prior to spawning. However, when nature calls, the females interests turn to spawning. I have heard of a few rare occasions where anglers caught females that had males thrashing at their sides all the way up to the boat. In most cases, you cannot entice the female with any offering while spawning. The time span may last about three days, and all do not spawn at the same time. So fishing for the females becomes spotty.

B4   LAKES DURING SPRING; Spawn
Still-Fishing

With the patience of a watchmaker, some old-timers rely on hotspots they have found, claimed, and depended on for years. The female finds holding spots while going to and retreating from her spawning grounds. Occasionally an angler stumbles upon a spot or two. The best become reliable year after year.

The spot might be a small flat of rock just off a steep drop-off; it could be an area where sand and rocks meet; or a hole in the weed bed adjacent to prime spawning areas. The common denominator is: all the spots provide some type of cover.

The best way to find the holding areas is by spending a great deal of time on the water searching while staying in proximity to prime spawning areas. When a prospective area is found, set up shop. Anchor and fan-cast the area, retrieving very slowly. After catching a fish, cast back to the same spot, and let your bait sit. Wait it out, these fish do not come easy.

Fish between known spawning grounds and known summer hot-spots. Work the area with confidence. The fish are there . . . believe it! Believe in every cast you make. Think the fish into striking. Concentration is tough . . . but it works.

There are several "still-fishing" rigs that are pop-ular among fishermen. Some of the original rigs have lasted through the "lure-rush" age. The "Wolf-River Rig" designed specifically for rivers, is also useful in lake fishing *(see Section III,A6)*. Insert the hook into the minnows back, just behind the dorsal fin. The sinker holds the rig in place, while the minnow makes a desperate attempt to escape.

The Lindy Rig has its place among the top ranking still-fishing rigs. A slow retrieve or just allowing it to sit, is an effective method of using this rig.

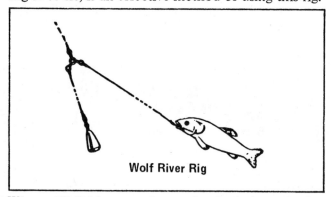

Wolf River Rig

When still-fishing, a minnow hooked through the back seems to work best. Other baits, such as the leech and nightcrawler can be used, and is more effective as water temperatures increase.

A floating jig and minnow has become very popular in recent years. The rig consists of a sinker, snell, floating jig and, usually, a minnow. In this case, hook the minnow through its mouth. The floating jig keeps the minnow off the bottom and makes it easier to see, especially near obstructions.

A lead-head jig is also used while still-fishing. The trick here is to hook the minnow through the mouth and not the middle of the head. Try to keep the minnow alive as long as possible. Hooking it through the head, of course, kills it. As the jig lies on the bottom, the minnow thrashes around trying to escape. It almost appears to be feeding on the jig. The action attracts attention. The walleye picks up the minnow and jig when striking. Try it in your minnow bucket, notice how the minnow acts. It looks great!

Still-fishing can be very rewarding if practiced with expectations of catching fish and not used as a way to get out of work.

C1   LAKES DURING SPRING; Post-Spawn
Cooperative Males

The males are actively feeding throughout the pre-spawn, spawn and post-spawn period. Walleyes in the one to three pound range are commonly caught. This makes fishing worth while. These fish are an excellent size for the table, and fun to catch.

As water temperatures rise, males make their way to deeper water. The visits to shallow water to feed are quite regular for a period of one to three weeks. There is an abundance of food in the shallows.

Perch spawn when water temperatures reach approximately fifty-two degrees. They will spend a considerable amount of time in shallow water. This sets up an excellent food base for the walleye. Occasionally large walleye are caught near the perch spawning areas.

Finally, after about a month in the shallows (counting pre-spawn, spawn and post-spawn) the males start to head for deeper waters. Schools start to scatter and fishing becomes tough.

C2   LAKES DURING SPRING; Post-Spawn
Post-Spawn Methods

Before males disperse they can be readily caught by any number of methods. Location of the males is the prime factor. Once found, a fisherman can usually catch a few fish almost immediately. The males are quite agressive under low-light conditions. The low-light conditions are: dark over-cast days; windy days, that cut down light penetration into the water; the darkness of depth (a steep drop-off); the cover of obstructions, weeds, timber, and rocks; the darkness of night, etc. The security of cover is important to the walleye.

Fish in the areas that are near the prime spawning grounds. Use small live-bait and lures. A good choice of live-bait is a golden shiner (small size); a fathead minnow about two inches long; a mudminnow in darker waters; a small chub or lake shiner. Leeches and nightcrawlers are better after a long spell of warm weather.

Use the lightest weight possible that will still take the bait to the bottom. A small number 8 or 10 hook is sufficient. Keep it simple.

When trolling with artificials use imitation minnows. At this time of year they are better producers than most other artificials. Make sure that the lure is working at the depth that you would like to cover, even if it means adding weight to the line to get it down.

In Upper Michigan I had a chance to talk to a fellow that was the area "expert". He showed me his trolling rigs. I could hardly believe the huge sized sinkers that were attached to his line just in front of the lure he was using. Yet he had caught many fish, some really decent, on this set-up. His theory is when fishing active fish, the weight hardly makes a difference, but, you must be at the correct depth to find active schools of walleyes. When times are tough, he changes his entire style of fishing, going back to good basic fishing habits.

Once the school is found, you can usually take a few fish before the action slows down. While changing lures will help to get a few more, it is better to find other active schools. If you want to concentrate on a particular school, don't lose the exact spot where fish contact had been made. Often times, the school is still active, but the fisherman moves off of his spot (even just a little) and loses the interest of the schools feeding fish. Throw out a marker, check out the area to find out what kind of structure you are on. Stay a jump ahead of the school. Figure out where the school might move to, if it does move. Then fish other areas that have the same type of structure at the same depth.

As water temperatures rise, and the schools of fish start to disperse, start concentrating on deeper water. Fishing will slow down but you will still catch some active fish.

C3   LAKES DURING SPRING; Post-Spawn
Scattered reluctant females

Virtually depleted of energy from spawning, the female makes her way back to the safety of deeper water. Enroute, she will feed on tidbits that take little energy to capture. Reluctantly, the female may hold the bait in its mouth before consuming it. To the fisherman, it is just a feeling of added weight on the line. As soon as the walleye feels the line tightening up she drops the offering. It becomes a game and is very aggravating. Particular attention is paid to the smell of the bait, the size of hook and weight on the line. It's tough to convince a weary female. She is lazy and will not expend excess energy in her quest for food.

The period of time between beginning post-spawn and early summer is a transitional period broken down into three distinct stages. Each stage is controlled by temperature changes and time (which we have no control over).

The first stage of transition occurs right after spawning. The walleye is feeding reluctantly. While moving to a deep water haunt, feeding slows down. An occasional catch is made in deep water. The females are scattered and don't seem to be holding to any particular pattern.

During the second stage of transition, the females are relatively deep, scattered and very tough to locate. A fisherman may not catch more than one fish out of a spot. The males also become tough to locate and catch. Walleye fishing in general is poor. This is a post-spawn condition.

The third stage of transition is when the walleyes re-group and set-up in their summer patterns. Re-grouping is not a regimented plan (if it were, we could credit them with the gift of thought and communication). Re-grouping happens naturally as the walleye seeks its food. There is a slow movement to the shallows again, and fishing becomes terrific. This happens during the summer period, not according to a calendar date, but to the warmer temperatures. Usually during the beginning of June in the upper third of the country.

During the post-spawn period catching walleyes requires a lot of skill. Slow methods with live bait takes a fish now and then, but face facts: walleyes are not active all of the time, so feel proud to bring in a fish or two.

D1 LAKES DURING SUMMER; Early Summer
Where Have All The Walleyes Gone?

All is not lost during the second stage of transition. During my research, I have discovered some interesting facts that will enable fishermen to catch walleyes even under the most difficult of conditions. Just remember this: walleyes must live near its food supply. In some lakes there is a splitting of walleye population which results in the presence of two and possibly three distinct groups of fish. All are walleyes, but live in different areas according to their food supply. Some walleyes take up residency in shallow water, usually in or near weeds or other cover providing structures.

The migratory walleye, is usually found moving from deep water to shallow water to feed and follows the shallow water food base.

Finally, there is the deep water walleye that is usually found in lakes that support a substantial suspended forage fish population (typically, lakes that support trout). The deep water walleye stays in proximity to its suspended forage. It comes in shallow to spawn in spring and follows the fall spawning forage into the shallows during late fall (Refer to *Section II, E7 and Section II, I3*).

The shallow water walleye remains in the weeds, even during the tough transition period. At night, while researching, I have always found some walleyes in the weeds, even during the toughest fishing periods. The shallow water resident is usually a loner and at best shares an area with less than a handfull of other walleyes. The exception is during the prime shallow water periods when most of the walleye population is in the shallows. The shallow water walleye is, percentage wise, a larger fish. The weeds offer food, cover and protection from other predators.

The weed walleye or shallow water fish is usually much darker than their open water cousins. For instance, on Lake Winnebage (a large body of water in Wisconsin), the split occurs between the migratory fish and the shallow water fish. Fishermen catch walleyes off of the reefs in 4 to 10 feet of water. They are usually light in color and have bright white bellies. Meanwhile, on the same lake and the same day, fishermen will occasionally catch some very dark colored walleyes having yellow tinted bellies in super shallow water. The only difference is that one lives in shallow water and takes on its coloration, while the other one lives in deeper water and migrates to the reefs, many times

WEED WALLEYE (top) is nearly as dark as the accompanying sauger.

following the sheepshead around. Consequently, lures such as the "Sparkle-Tail" and "Rapala" are very popular on the reefs.

In comparing notes with veteran guide, Mike Baranowski, owner of the Sunset Cove Camp in Nestor Falls, Ontario (on The Lake of the Woods); Mike has noticed the distinct difference for years. At times his guides fish for walleyes in twenty or thirty feet of water and on the same day catch some walleyes in super shallow water. The color of the walleyes is completely different. The deep water fish are usually very light in color, while the shallow water fish are very dark. Mike is convinced that those big shallow water hogs can be caught in the weeds during August also (usually a time of deep water fishing).

At night the shallow water walleye becomes quite active. It roams around and above the shoreline weeds. During seven years of research at night, I have almost always seen some walleye in the shallow water weeds.

Percentage wise, the split is very uneven *(Section II, 13)*. If all three co-exist in the same body of water, the deep water fish will be most abundant on a deep water lake. The ingredients necessary for a natural split are: an abundant population of suspended forage (cisco, whitefish, etc.); a large expanse of weeds along the shoreline (and in some cases, timber); and a shallow water food base where there is a lack of cover.

In the first ingredient, a deep water food base draws the walleye to inhabit the deeper waters. In the second, the weeds and timber provide a shallow water food base for small fish, in turn, the shallow water walleye. In the third case, the walleye migrates up to its food (on shoreline areas as well as bars), feeds, and returns to the security of deep water.

In each case the common denominators are the food base, and the security of cover. The best fishing occurs when both the migrant walleye and the shallow water walleye occupy relatively shallow water. This happens during the spawning period of spring; the summer period (the third stage of transition); a brief period in early fall; and again during late fall, just before ice-up. The deep water walleye will also be in relatively shallow water during spawning time and late fall, when the forage spawns (its food).

There are two ways of handling the tough fishing period. One is to work for the deep water fish, fishing near known walleye spots, or; fishing at night for the shallow water fish (if that fishery is on the lake that you're fishing). The night fishing methods are discussed in *Section II E7*.

D2. LAKES DURING SUMMER; Early Summer Fishing Under Tough Conditions

For some fishermen, tough conditions seem to prevail during every fishing trip. I hope to change that. "Tough Conditions" are the set of circumstances that makes the joy of catching fish a task. The following is a list of tough conditions and solutions to the problems.

TOUGH CONDITIONS

1. Strong gusty winds
2. High pressure system
3. No wind
4. Clear water
5. Lake activity
6. Wind changes
7. Rocks, boulders and weeds
8. First day after a major weather change
9. Hard rain/lightning
10. Extremely deep or shallow water
11. Inadequate tools
12. An abundance of suspended forage

Tough condition . . . strong, gusty winds.

Strong winds are always a problem. Walleye fishing for the most part is a "bottom contact sport". Winds make it difficult to stay in contact with the bottom without going to over-sized weights and baits.

Possible solutions: anchor and use just enough weight to keep the bait on the bottom. Another is controlled trolling with lures that travel near the bottom or at the depth that is to be fished. Forward trolling offers better control in windy waters. Finding good available structure in less windy regions is another way to handle the situation.

Tough condition . . . high pressure system.

The effect of high pressure does not seem to be as drastic in deep water as it is in shallow waters. High pressure systems are usually accompanied with a bright sun and picturesque blue sky, the "hangover" of a frontal condition. High pressure with humid conditions tend to make the baitfish suspend a bit higher in the water; high pressure with little humidity puts them closer to the bottom (ask any live-bait trapper).

Possible solutions: Slow down, use thin diameter lines, longer leaders (where applicable), and just enough weight to put you in your prospective fish catching depth. When using live-bait, take all precautions avoiding human scent and use smaller baits. Still fish, experimenting with bait held at various levels.

Tough condition . . . no wind.

When it is calm there is greater light penetration into the water, it eliminates drift fishing entirely and has hampered the success of many walleye fishing trips. Be thankful that the condition is temporary.

Possible solution: Back-trolling offers an accurate form of boat control. Live bait should be back-trolled. Artificials should be trolled slowly, forward. The difference is: forward trolling with artificials allows you to cover a lot of territory finding active fish. Back-trolling offers precise control, needed to work a school of fish. With the additional light penetration accompanied by windless days, try fishing the shaded edges of cover. Fan-casting known walleye spots will also help. It is better to impart some action to your bait than letting it sit.

Tough condition . . . clear water.

You will probably have to fish deeper than normal. If fishing shallow, the cast must be long and if fish are present they will usually be found in or around obstructions.

Solution: Use artificial lures in shallow water where the cast must be long, due to water clarity. Use a bobber and live bait over weeds and shallow obstructions. If it is the period where fish are in deep water, no problem. Use methods that have been discussed. However, when fishing in a shallow water period, motor out to the point where the bottom disappears visually. Stay between that point and approximately ten feet deeper. This will give you an excellent starting point. Work the structure thoroughly. The greatest concentration of fish should be in this region.

Tough condition . . . lake activity.

To the fisherman, there's nothing worse than an armada of water skiers, cruisers and sail boaters that always seem to make use of the best fishing areas.

Solution: Spend more morning and evening hours on the lake. Plan your choice of lakes a little more closely or work the weeds for some of those shallow water walleyes. Everyone has water rights, so compromise and be courteous.

Tough condition . . . wind changes.

Often times wind changes are a sign of weather change. This condition could soon change to a favorable one.

Solution: Trolling seems to help. Walleyes tend to be less active during a high-pressure system; feed as a group during low pressure; and group tightly under windy situations. The change of wind may put fish on the move and create activity. Trolling will help to locate active fish.

Tough condition . . . rocks, boulder and weeds.

The rocks seem to snag anything that comes near them. Crayfish, leeches and other aquatic creatures find a wealth of food among them. The end result is, walleyes and other game fish inhabit the better rock shelves.

Solution: When using live-bait rigs, don't use heavy sinkers. Try some of the floating rigs, they work very well. Don't let out a lot of line. Try to position the boat right over the rocks and straight line it. When you get hung-up, back up just a bit and work your bait loose.

Use jigs that have wire hooks, so when pressure is added, the hook will bend enough to work it free. Get yourself a good supply of cheap jigs — you are going to lose some.

Troll with a Wolf-River Rig set-up. Use a small pound-test line from the three-way swivel to the weight. You might lose a sinker or two, but the expensive lure is usually saved.

Boulders are not as bad as rocks. However, the crevices can claim your live-bait and artificial lures just as easily.

Solution: Straight line it; troll with lures; or cast lures that will dive and bounce off the boulders. This creates enough sound to draw attention from fish. Another method is to use a water-fillable slip-bobber along with live-bait. Allow the slip-bobber to hold or suspend the live-bait just above the boulders. Cast to prospective spots and retrieve slowly. If you retrieve too fast the rig will rise in the water and not hold a proper depth pattern.

An exposed hook will find plenty of trouble in both weeds and timber. There are not that many walleye fishermen that realize the potential that lies in fishing for walleyes in the weeds. But it is worthwhile.

Solutions: At night, troll very slowly above the weeds with a Flikker Rig (no weight), or skim a Floating Rapala (see Section II,E7). During the day, use some of the weedless jigheads and powerhead jigs.

Try a simple bobber, split shot and live-bait combination. Set the bobber at a distance that will allow the bait to suspend at the tops of the weeds

ILLUSTRATION 105

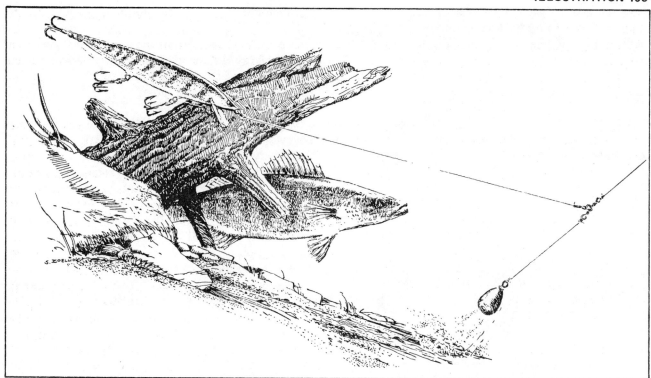

and work it slowly back to the boat.

Usually, near the end of weedbeds that extend in to deep water, there is a thinning in the weeds or sparse weed clumps. During summer, they are like magnets drawing walleye to them because of food and cover. A jig and minnow is an excellent choice. Artificials that dive to those depths are tempting to active fish.

Timber and brush seems nearly impossible to work. In certain situations, particularly rivers, walleyes will use them often.

Solution: A simple bobber, split-shot and live bait offers depth control, and that is the important factor.

Heavier diameter lines and jigs with wire hooks are a partial solution. The use of artificials is prob-

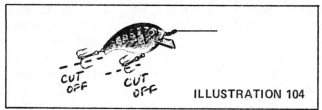

ILLUSTRATION 104

ably the easiest way to work timber. Pick out a deep-diving crankbait (even though you're working shallow water); hold it up vertically, so the treble hooks lie against the bait. Cut the exposed hook, do the same on the lower treble. That is the hook that catches onto everything; without it the lip digs downward and other hooks pass right over the obstacle. You will lose an occasional crank-bait, but not nearly as many as working with full hooking power. (See Illustration 104).

Tough condition . . . first day after a major weather change.

Major weather changes have a drastic affect on feeding habits of walleye. The change appears to put them into a nervous state of being. They are really turned off. The active fish are very finicky and reluctant to hit. An occasional fish is caught, but conditions are tough.

Solution: Stay in the known walleye spots. Use small diameter lines, live-bait and avoid human scent whenever possible. Smaller baits are best. Retrieves should be slow.

Tough condition . . . hard rain/lightning.

The sound of hard rain beating on the surface of the water makes fishing tough.

Solution: For safety reasons, get off the water. There is not a fish that is worth a possible mishap.

Tough condition . . . extremely deep or shallow water.

It is difficult to present a small lure or bait to a walleye that may be in forty or fifty feet of water. When the water is perfectly calm, a 1/4 ounce bait seems to take forever to reach the bottom. The slightest amount of wind moves the boat around, making the lure rise in the water, it also puts a bow in the line. Not to mention the fact that feeling plays an important part in walleye fishing. The telegraphic contact between fisherman and fish through the line is almost impossible at those depths when using light line and live-bait. Much has to be over-come when fishing in deep water.

Solution: When deep water is the problem, use larger sinkers to make bottom contact. Your leader length may be increased to work with minor depth changes. A short leader will hug the bottom; a longer (possible four to six feet) leader will help keep the bait further from the sinker, and tend to rise.

Small diameter line will also help. The less water resistance against the lure, the easier it is to keep the sinker on the bottom. These tactics will help when using live-bait while still-fishing or slowly drifting over deep water.

Motor-trolling with live or artificial bait can be very productive. Use a three-way-swivel, drop-sinker and bait combination *(See Illustration 105)* to keep the sinker at the bottom and your bait a-bove it. Wire line cuts the water and has weight, the result is trolling deeper without excess line behind the boat. Productive shallow water is usually filled to the hilt with obstructions. Proper present-ation is difficult. Rocks, boulders, weeds and tim-ber have been discussed earlier. Common sense tells you when it is practical to fish the shallows. Low light-level hours are best, morning, evening and at night. A chop on the water is best during

the daylight hours if accompanied with a cloudy sky.

Solution: Choose the time of day, and weather conditions that favor fishing in the shallows. Then choose lures or live-bait accordingly.

Tough condition . . . inadequate tools.

A mismatch in rod, reel, line and lures causes more failures than any of the other items in the "tough conditions" catagory. There's an entire section in this book devoted to matching equip-ment and getting the proper tools. Various situa-tions call for different diameter lines, size of lures, time of year for the use of lures, special purpose rods, etc.

Solution: Sit down and examine your fishing. Figure out which methods play an important role in almost every fishing trip. Build your equipment around those methods. If you need to expand — get the proper equipment and use it for the specific reasons that you purchased it for. This will aid in self-discipline and sticking to your game plan.

Tough condition . . . abundance of forage.

Almost every walleye fisherman has a lake that has got tons of wall-hangers in it. Every spring, they catch a few big fish and see hundreds of them spawning. But afterwards they don't see another walleye all year. These types of lakes are usually loaded with suspended forage, maybe some trout and possibly very clear water; or they are infested with weeds. These conditions are hard to fight. Suspended forage offers unlimited feeding oppor-tunities for the walleye. The suspended forage might be cisco, tullibee, whitefish, alewife, shad or other members of the herring family.

Solution: Walleyes will be in relatively shallow waters and accessible to the fisherman during two times of the year. One is during spawning, the other is in late fall when the suspended forage spawns. The walleye will follow the forage to shal-low waters. They always stay in proximity to their food.

You must face the fact that it will be tough to catch walleyes out of these lakes, don't marry the lake unless you live on it.

Another solution (a very slow process) is to find

the suspended forage level-of-concentration and fish the structures where that depth and the structure meets. A depth finder or graph is essential. This will usually be in deep water where there is sufficient oxygen content. Some walleyes have been caught out of ninety feet of water on these types of lakes during the latter part of summer.

Early summer is considered to be the second stage transition period. The females are usually deep, scattered (slight grouping does occur), and tougher to locate than to catch. There is an occasional shallow water fish caught, usually at night. Steep drop-offs that are adjacent to both spawn areas and known summer hotspots are the areas to concentrate on. If a saddle is present, work back and forth between structures. After catching a fish, spend a little time working the spot . . . but not too long; ten minutes or so is long enough then move on.

D3   LAKES DURING SUMMER; Early Summer Anchoring

The anchor is a potent, valuable tool in the hands of an aggressive fisherman. Before anchoring, give some thought to the area and depth that you wish to work. The anchor can be a very useful tool in positioning the boat; holding the boat, or finding a drop-off. It can be used to hold the boat in position or as a pivot point in the wind . . . and put you in a fishless position if you're careless.

During early summer, you will be fishing in deeper water trying to locate some of those lazy females, or a school of males. In *Illustration 106* there are four diagrams. Wind and the depth of water to be fished will help to determine which will fit your situation. In *Fig. 1,* the anchor is lowered into deep water from both the bow and stern of the boat. The wind and drag of the anchor will lock you into position. From this position fisherman (1) and (3) can work the dropoff and fisherman (2) can cast towards the shallows, covering different depths of water. If fish are not located within fifteen minutes or so, move on. You're looking for active fish! If the wind is relatively light, and the dropoff is to be fished, *Fig.(2)* offers the same potential as *Fig. (1),* except the an-

chor position is less likely to spook fish. Fishermen (1) and (2) can cast into deep water and bring the bait back up the dropoff. *Fig. (3)* offers greater versatility in working the water. Use the wind to your advantage. The single anchor will work as a pivot point, swinging the boat, allowing you to cover more water thoroughly. As in *Fig.(3)* you might anchor at the tip of a gravel bar and swing back and forth covering both dropoffs. Straight-line jigging, fan-casting or just retrieving the bait slowly, are some of the methods that can be used. In *Fig. (4)* the fishermen know where the bar is and go upwind of it. They lower the anchors down twenty feet or so and drift toward the bar. They can fan-cast toward the bar or just drift with the lines out. The anchors will eventually catch, the shallow water should be worked thoroughly. It is also a good way of locating other bars if one is without a depth finder.

E1   LAKES DURING SUMMER: Summer The Walleye Bonanza

The sun-bathers are schooling on sandy beaches and the walleye are setting up in their summer patterns. A beautiful combination. The third stage of transition is here. The males and females are starting to school and hunt for food, but not together. In most cases when a school of walleye is located, most of the fish look like they were cut from the same mold with little variation in size. At times you will catch a number of males, then the action slows, and suddenly a few larger females are caught. I have experienced this a number of times.

The underwater islands and shoreward structures seem to come alive with walleyes. Not all of them, just the ones that provide a good food base for the walleye. The long slopes are used more now. The steep dropoffs are associated with cold water fishing. The short breaks are also used, if a good food shelf lies above them.

A contour map will help to set up a game plan. To get an idea of some of the potential fish catching areas, take a look at *Illustration 107*. Area (A) is a long flat that has a thick weedbed on the shallow side and tapers off into deep water. The deeper side of the flat has clumps of weeds extend-

ILLUSTRATION 106

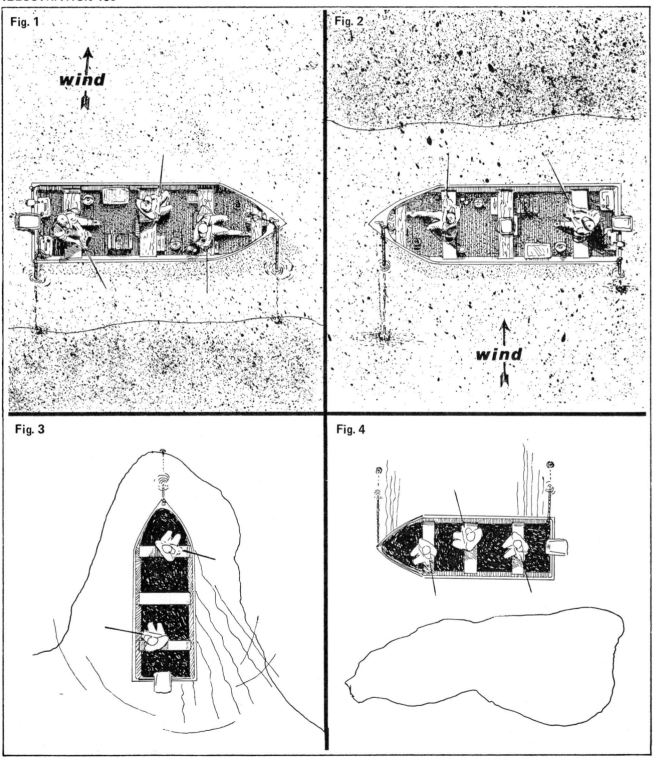

ILLUSTRATION 107

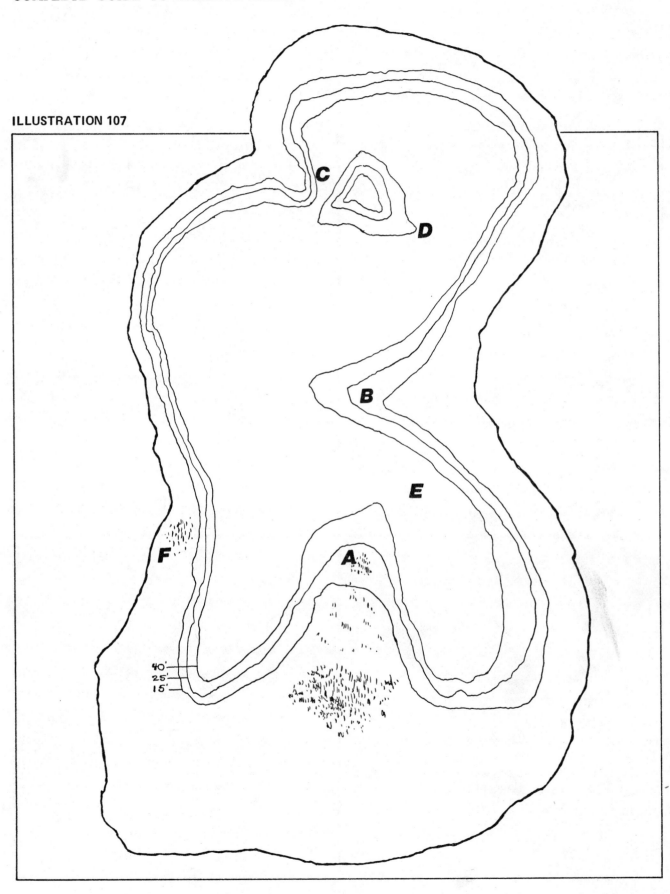

ing into deep water. The weeds provide a food base for smaller fish and in turn draw the walleyes to them. The area between (A) and (E) could be a saddle if the distance between the two is less than one hundred yards. If you should find action at (E), spend a lot of time between the two structures. Point (B) could be very good when associated with gravel, rocks and most importantly, food. It stretches towards the deepest part of the lake and is the main structure in the area. The natural saddle created by (C) could show fish catching potential all year long. The flat (D) coming off of the underwater bar has great potential but a food shelf must exist. These are the likely spots for summer movement of walleye. There could be many others present, created by the fact that a food base is present.

Current is a natural fish attractor. Should there be an inlet, spend a great deal of your time working at the dropoff that is near it. Current usually means food, oxygen and cover. The three ingredients essential to the walleye.

E2   LAKES DURING SUMMER: Summer Schooling Fish

During various stages of its life, the walleye feeds on various foods that are important to its existence during those stages. As fish grow, their food preferences change, creating distinct groups or schools searching for favored or needed foods. In other words, six inch walleyes would not have the same food item desires (on a constant basis) as a six pound walleye. As a matter of fact, the six pound walleye may eat the six inch fish!

When in the one to three pound bracket, schools are usually large. When larger fish roam, you could call them "groups" of fish, rather than "schools"; because their numbers are usually substantially less. Occasionally there will be a very successful hatch of a certain year class. A few years later, the lake will have an abundance of decent sized fish. Some of those females become loners because they became a major predator in their own right and work feeding grounds that suit their particular needs.

This is a good thing to remember when you're looking for big fish. The schools are not as abundant as the smaller males, and at times they need methods that require the use of larger bait. I know of a few fishermen who are strictly big-fish fishermen. They catch a few big fish each year (over ten or twelve pounds) because of their persistence in non-conventional methods. In order to catch big fish somewhat consistently you must have big fish knowledge; be able to locate big fish; be familiar with some of the un-conventional methods, practice them, and; be on a big fish lake. The last item might seem a little humorous, but some anglers are convinced that all lakes that have walleyes also have a lot of big fish. It's not necessarily true.

BIG FISH KNOWLEDGE allowed Dan Sura to catch this string of huge walleyes. The largest fish of the group weighs over sixteen pounds.

Some environments are not conducive to producing big walleye. Make sure that a number of big fish have been caught in the lake that you are fishing, or spawning runs show a substantial number of huge walleyes. Then remember that they are concentrated during the spawning run and could be very difficult to locate when searching over the vast expanse of a lake or flowage.

E3   LAKES DURING SUMMER; Summer
         Fishing For Numbers of Fish

The average fisherman will be quite satisfied if he brings home frying-pan size fish. Most of the walleyes will be one to three pound fish and those are nice walleyes. A stringer of fish weighing one to three pounds looks darn good and feeds more than a few mouths. The areas that are shown by *Illustration 107* will give you a good starting point. Knowledge of fair to good conditions is a critical factor. Many fishermen don't recognize where good conditions exist. It is an empty feeling to come off the lake without fish, especially when the walleyes are really active.

In this section I will explain what some of the better conditions are, and methods used to increase your catches.

A ripple on the water: the light penetration is cut down with a ripple, more so with a good chop. Go to the windy side of the lake and work the best structures available.

Medium water color: fishing lakes with medium to dark water coloration will help to give you some versatility in methods to be used. Fishing clear water lakes is tough. I don't mean to give you the impression that you should not fish clear bodies of water; but if you have a choice in the matter, look for darker water. Some clear bodies of water have areas of darker water. Fish them. Fish deep in clear water and shallow in medium to dark water.

Low light conditions: spend more time fishing the early mornings, evenings and nights. A lot of fish catching is done during those times. The exception is cloudy days; an overcast is good.

Stable wind: If winds have the waves pounding the west shore (or any shore), fish the best structure available on the west side of the lake. There is usually a build up of plankton, drawing bait-fish, and active game fish.

Gravel, sand and sparse weeds: look for structure that is connected to deep water. Find the bait-fish, they are the magnets that draw walleye. Have a purpose for every area that you fish.

Change of barometric pressure: quick pressure changes seem to turn fish on. Fish in your known walleye spots during pressure changes. The fish should become active.

Major weather changes: as a general rule, the first day after a major weather change is usually terrible. On the second day there is a slight improvement with some fish being caught. From the third day on, fishing will improve greatly.

Drizzle or mist: a slight drizzle or mist is accompanied by lower light conditions and this is good. I have caught many walleyes while out in the rain. I have not caught one during a hard rain, unless there was a lot of wind.

Medium depth of water: the times of the year that the greatest amount of the walleye populations are in mid-depths is the best times to fish. Plan trips around favorable conditions. Year after year I used to plan my longer trips to coincide with the opening of the walleye fishing season. The largemouth bass would be very active, smallmouth bass pretty active, and even a few muskies, but walleyes were tough unless the trip was on a river system. Early summer and late fall have been much more productive.

Little or no suspended forage and a good shoreline food base: lakes that have an abundance of suspended forage are much tougher to fish than ones that don't. If there is little suspended forage, walleyes have to spend more time near the shoreline and bars. When there is much competition for food, walleye fishing is easier. Research the lakes that you plan to spend some time on. Proper preparation will save you a lot of frustration.

Predators: "My lake is loaded with walleyes but not one ever catches them!" We have all heard of that before. Normally there are three practical explanations: either the lake has a lot of suspended forage; it's loaded to the hilt with northern pike or muskie; or the lake has more weeds than deep water. Northern pike and muskie have a drastic effect on the location and feeding habits of the walleye. At times they will force the walleye to move a lot or find safety in the weeds.

Some guides will attest to that. They will catch a fish or two from a school, the action will stop and then they will catch a northern or muskie. Then they must locate another school of walleye. The affect is greatest on walleyes up to about four pounds. Walleyes that are over four pounds also become major predators within the lake. This, in some lakes, may change their location patterns entirely. Stomach contents have revealed an assortment of tidbits above the normal items, they include: bullheads, crayfish, leeches, aquatic insects, frogs, salamanders, smaller walleye, (one fourteen pounder had a fourteen inch walleye in it) perch, bluegills, crappies, and northern pike (one fish that I had caught was about three pounds and had a northern pike in it that was six inches long). This does not mean that these items represent the sought-after food base, it merely points out the location the walleyes must have been in to be able to feed on the items.

So, when fishing for numbers of fish, the male is the primary target. The schools are larger, there are more of them, and there is a greater variety of baits that can be used to catch them.

After marking down potential spots on the map comes the job of researching the lake. Motor to the spots that you have marked on your map. Ride the contour and get a feel for the lake. See if spot (A) on the map is actually a long point with rocks, check the bars and look for cover such as rocks, weeds or gravel. Take notice to see if there is a lot of bait-fish in the area. Get information from the natives, ask where some of the known walleye spots are and search out areas that have similarities. Get to know the lake before you actually fish it. Plan to spend some time on each of the potential areas.

With a plan in mind, start your fishing. You can cover more water if you have another person in the boat. One fisherman might start with a Lindy Rig and another with a jig and minnow. If you're geared to forward trolling, make sure that you and your partner are using different lures. The object

is to find out what is working best at that particular time. Try to find active fish. After locating some active fish, keep using the productive baits until the fishing slows down, then quickly change colors, size and expand on location a bit.

Don't over-fish the school. Move to another of the spots that you have planned to spend some time on. Finding a number of spots with active fish on will keep you in fish for a long time to come. Knowing when to move is a key to successful fishing. Hint: when the walleyes start short striking and playing with the bait, move.

E4   LAKES DURING SUMMER; Summer
        Fishing For Large Fish

You have caught your share of small walleyes and are ready for some hog-hunting. Dreams of the wall-hanger linger in your minds-eye. Extremely large walleyes are usually caught during early spring (before spawning) or late fall for that's when they weigh the most. Fewer are caught during summer. Location during summer varies with the time period, because late summer fishing is usually done in deep water. The period we are covering now is one where the walleyes are quite active and relatively shallow (the third stage of transition).

Fishing for large walleye is tough to begin with because (1) you are fishing for a less abundant fish; (2) fishing for smaller groups of fish; and (3) a fish that may have adapted to feeding on a greater variety of foods.

Generally, I have not found too much of a depth difference (with the exception of the shallow water walleye) between small fish and large fish; most of the time within ten feet of depth difference. Occasionally I have found a large school of small fish occupying a gravel flat in fifteen feet of water and have found large females grouping at about twenty-five feet on the same structure. Seldom have I found both groups together; but have had the smaller walleye action slow down and begin to catch some larger fish.

More "bits and pieces": I have caught some larger walleyes over mud flats during this time of the year as well as late summer. The insect hatches commonly associated with mud flats has appeared as a mass or glob in some of those large walleyes stomachs, indicating some feed on them.

While grouping occurs in deeper water, the shallow water walleye (the weed walleye) appears to be a loner, where the abundance of food may draw a few to an area. While researching at night, I witnessed a few large fish scattered over an area of possibly more than fifty yards of weeds, and a number of smaller fish in the same areas.

The key to walleye location is an abundance of food located at or near cover. Many publications have unintentionally led the fisherman to believe that all walleyes relate to some sort of dropoff. Of course a great percentage of the walleyes do. However, if it were true of all small fish and large fish, then there would be more big fish catches than you could shake a stick at. Fishermen would bring in at least a number of stringers of four to eight pound fish, quite common in most of our better walleye waters. But they don't! And they don't because the walleyes feeding habits change and this effects the location of fish.

It is much harder for a ten pound walleye to chase down small minnows than a two pound fish. It takes a greater amount of food to satisfy the bigger female. The result is to feed on easier and larger prey.

The most successful big fish fishermen that I know spend most of their time fishing with large live-bait or large artificial bait on flowages and river systems. Some are strictly night fishermen. True, some big fish catches are made while fishing for smaller fish, but as far as consistency, the big fish fisherman has a better chance over a given period of time.

During this time period, the chub that is between three and six inches long, the leech, and salamanders have a more than fair chance of attracting a large walleye. The chub is active, tough and easy to use. I prefer to use it with a single hook rather than making it appear unnatural with two and three hook rigs. There are two basic ways of hooking the chub; a single hook through the mouth (not the head because you will kill it), if I am going to drift or troll, or behind the dorsal fin if still-fishing. Use a number four or six hook.

A TREMENDOUS CATCH of walleyes from Gull Lake, Minnesota. The walleyes, ranging in size from 6½ to 9½ pounds were taken on salamanders on a live bait rig. And, yes, that's Al Lindner with the big smile.

Leeches are tough; natural in most of our lakes; active during warm water periods; and attractive to all sizes of walleye. The size of leech can make a difference. Small leeches are not as well accepted as large ones by larger walleye. It is best to hook the leech through the fat end, right at the sucker. When hooked through the thin end the leech will occasionally wind around the line. Leeches have a ribbon-like motion that is very enticing. Walleyes really like them.

To save money purchase a pound of leeches. Keep them in a cooler or refrigerator at or below fifty degrees. They need a little oxygen and the water should be changed about once every three days. They can live for a long time without being fed, some up to a year.

I have seen fishermen using rubber gloves, pliers and all sorts of instruments when hooking a leech.

They are not needed. I have handled leeches for more than ten years and have not gotten bitten nor have I had blood drawn by them. It feels a bit uncomfortable when handling leeches and occasionally they will stick to your hand, but they are easily pulled off. The biggest problem with leeches is that they cannot tolerate the heat and die quickly in a container that is left out in the sun.

Salamanders are great to use if you get them through the northern pike. That can be expensive if you purchase your "sallies". The best size sallie that I have found is between six and eight inches from head to tip of the tail. Sallies are tough and can be used over again. Make sure that you bring them up for air about once very fifteen minutes. Just bring them to the surface and let them descend again. Use them when the bottom is gravel, sand or mud. In the weeds they will grab everything in sight or bury themselves. Hook them through the mouth when drifting or trolling and through the base of the tail when still-fishing. A sharp forged hook, number four or six will be sufficient.

Grab the salamander right behind the head. I have not been bitten by a salamander, but its poor eyesight might lend a helping hand in mistaking a finger for food. Purchase them in 1/2 or dozen lots and keep them in a container in a dark cool place. I feed them grubs, wax worms, nightcrawlers, or minnows. You should keep some food in with them or they will bit each others legs and tail off. Walleyes strike violently at the salamander, at times carrying it off much like a muskie would do. I make a practice to allow them plenty of time when using large live bait. After the fish stops moving pick up your slack and set the hook.

In some states it is legal to use a part of your creel limit as bait. Using perch as bait can be very productive when other baits are not available. The best size of perch (for big fish) is about six to eight inches long. Take a scissors and cut the dorsal fin down to about a 1/2 inch. Insert the hook into the perches mouth. The perch will have a hard time stabilizing and look wounded. Cutting the tail works also. For smaller fish I have cut perch bellies and used the white undersides very effectively.

A 1/4th ounce sinker will usually do the job with these baits unless fishing deeper than twenty-five feet, or during strong winds. Try to keep the bait at or very close to the bottom.

The use of large artificial baits can be employed when the walleyes are active and in less than twenty-five feet of water. When over twenty-five feet, presentation of the lures is extremely difficult. Muskie size plugs should be trolled just off the structures or over mud bottoms. The largest

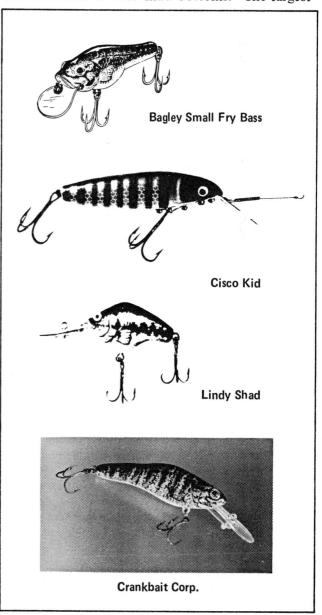

Bagley Small Fry Bass

Cisco Kid

Lindy Shad

Crankbait Corp.

spoonplug runs approximately twenty-five feet deep and can be trolled slowly without losing action. Other lures such as the large Bagley, Cisco Kid, Lindy Shad, and Crankbait Corp. lures are trolled, occasionally bumping bottom with slow to medium speeds. When trolling fast you will usually pick up more northern pike than walleye.

A snap swivel does not seem to affect the number of strikes, and allows the lure to react to water dynamics without restraining the action.

Fish an area rather than a spot. The grouping of larger fish is a lot looser than smaller fish. Occasionally you will find a tight school but it is rare. Extend over the base of a structure rather than hugging it unless it is a different time period than summer. At night I have found skimming to be productive (this is discussed in *Section II, E7).*

E5   LAKES DURING SUMMER; Summer
       Structures And How To Fish Them

When applied to fishing, the definition of structure is as follows: that which is different from its surroundings, having the capability of holding or attracting fish. Some examples are: a rock on a smooth flat; a certain dropoff; the thermocline; a separation of clear water and dark water; a weedbed; the level at which bait-fish are found on that particular day, etc.

As you can see, some structures are easily recognized and others take a bit of looking into. A "break" is: the dropoff or any recognizable change in depth in the lake. A "break-line" is a stretch along the dropoff or break. The breakline could also refer to the location of change in water temperature or coloration. It may seem confusing at first, but most of the terms are used in sentences or conversations that qualify their meanings.

Other than a boat, there are two basic tools that every fisherman should have. One is a depth finder and the other is a set of marker buoys. New electronic depth finders are best and take little of your time. The old sinker (lead weight) and string is a tough way to go, and time consuming. The most reliable units that I have worked with are the Lowrance and Humminbird. If you don't own a boat, then the Lowrance 300-D portable unit is an excellent choice. They have been around for a long time and have the bugs worked out of them. They became the first truly acceptable and broadly marketed unit available. If you own your boat, then either the Lowrance 360 or Humminbird Super Sixty are an excellent choice. Learn to read the depth finder. It is your eyes to the world below you. It doesn't lie. If there are fish indicated, they are there! You will be able to identify the type of bottom; find out if there are fish close to the bottom; in some instances tell where the thermocline is; and find the bait-fish in-between. It is a must for the serious angler.

Marker buoys will help to give you a visual picture of the structure to be fished. Structures are easy to plot and the markers come in handy for marking a spot where a fish has been caught. You can make your own, but the ones on the market are decent and don't cost that much. Round ones are the least desirable, especially in a wind. They tend to unravel and give you a poor picture of the structure that you are actually fishing. The best ones are flat, manufactured by Lowrance, Humminbird and Lindy. The flat ones are stable in the wind and quite reliable.

Carry about a dozen markers, paint two of them with a different color, so you will have two markers that can be used for marking certain parts of the break. I'll explain more later. Marking the break is time consuming. You might plot out ten or more breaks during a day of fishing when fish are hard to locate. But it is time well spent!

The structure is marked according to the way in which it is to be fished. If fishing the deep side, the markers are dropped on the shallow side. If working the shallow side, the markers are dropped on the deep side. When fishing a dropoff at the edge of a weedbar, the markers are put in on the deep side. Refer to *Illustration 108 Fig. (1).* Motor along the point to get a general idea of its shape. Then determine where your efforts will be centered. Will you fish the top of the break; both sides, with the shade side first; the deeper water at the base; the tip of the point; or up one side and down the other? Time of year and water clarity will help in answering those questions. If you are confused and don't really know what position the

ILLUSTRATION 108

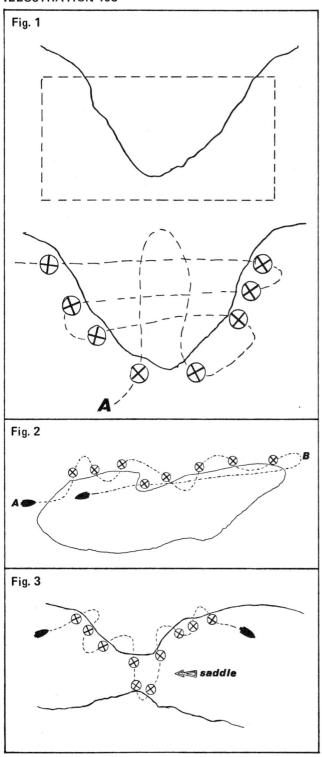

Fig. 1

Fig. 2

Fig. 3

saddle

fish are in at that particular time, then mark the entire point using the deep water as your guide.

If the structure is a steep dropoff, use twenty feet as your dropping point. If it is a slope use fifteen feet unless there is a weedbed, then use twenty feet. In *Fig. (1A);* start at (A); motor toward the break, drop a marker at twenty feet and continue through then make a sharp turn with your boat. Drop another marker when you reach twenty feet again. Swing the boat to one side and come back over the side of the point, drop another marker at twenty feet and go across the point and mark that. Continue until you have dropped at least eight markers. Now motor along the inside of the markers and drop the odd colored markers wherever you find a little inside turn or piece of structure that seems a bit different. They could be the best fish holding spots.

There are a number of ways to fish this point. You can motor-troll along the inside of the markers; position the boat outside the markers and cast just above the dropoff and work the bait down; position above the break in shallow water and work your baits up the dropoff; still-fish at the point; fish the shady side, etc.

In *Fig. (2)* a stretch of the break or an underwater gravel bar represents the area to be fished. Motor along the break to get an idea of how the break runs. You will be surprised at how much you will discover on lakes that you feel you had already known. Start at (A) and move in and out dropping the markers at fifteen or twenty feet of depth. Save those odd colored ones for running the inside of the markers. At times you will find a finger that runs in a bit further than the rest of the break. You will also find some flats that run out a bit further. These are key areas, they are something that is different from the surroundings.

Saddles are important, they can be some of the year-long hotspots. There are a number of ways to plot out the saddle in *Fig. (3).* If the ridges or points of the saddle run within a reasonable distance of each other, you can plot both at the same time; if not, just mark the closest point on one side and fully mark the other. The deep water between the saddle often times represent daytime holding areas. After fishing the marked off side, mark out

ILLUSTRATION 108

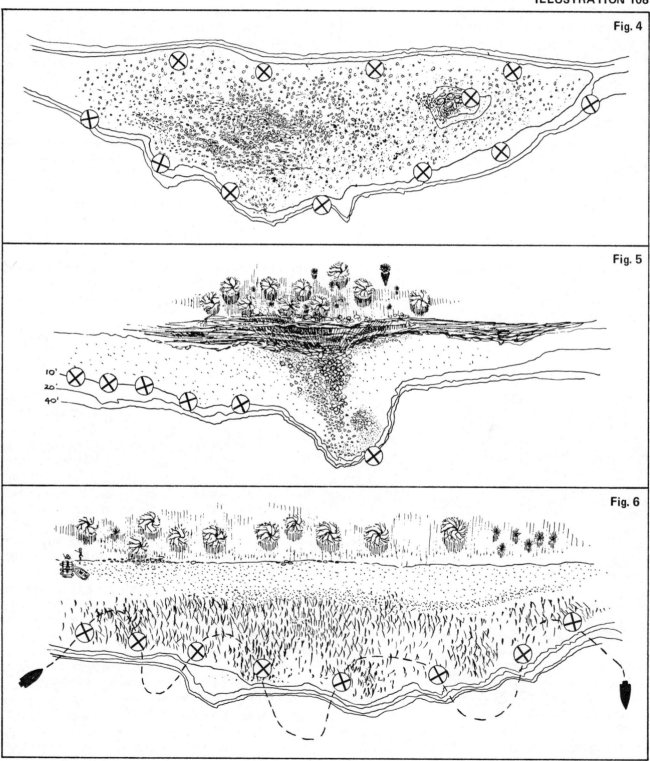

Fig. 4

Fig. 5

Fig. 6

the other portion and fish it.

Marking out a gravel bottom is a bit more difficult. First the marriage between you and your
depth finder must be a close one. You have to understand what it's telling you. The gravel bar or
hard bottom area may be at the bottom or base of
some structure; or just out in deeper water without
a connection to other structures.

In most cases, there is a slight rise even on a pre-
sumably flat gravel structure. Use the odd colored
markers to indicate the rise. Find the side of the
gravel bar that is closest to a break, mark it (your
markers might be in thirty or forty feet of water).
Run the edge of the gravel bar and mark the areas
where there is a change in the bottom reading. Use
all of your markers to do it. These are the areas
that represent potential, although the flats may be
occupied at times. There are many options available to fish it; it can be trolled; back-trolled; drifted; cast to; jigged; or just still-fished.

For the most part, cliffs (Fig. 5) are associated
with cold water fishing. Towering sheets of rock
may be fifty feet or higher, looking like downtown
Chicago. There are certain sections of rock that
are better than others. Look at the bases and seek
out areas where there is a large amount of broken
rock at the base. Often times these broken rock
areas extend below the surface and follow suit towards the bottom. Motor along a prospective area
and look for irregularities on the bottom, indicating broken rock. These areas attract crayfish and
other aquatic creatures. Motor along the first major break and drop your markers along the inside
edge (usually fifteen feet or shallower), just above
the dropoff. Use the odd colored markers to indicate points, or rock slides.

A successful method has been to cast a jig and
minnow into the shallows and retrieve it to the
break, letting it free-fall toward the bottom. This
can be accomplished by opening your bail and letting line out. Often times the strike is on the fall.
So watch your line for the slightest twitch. Trolling with a live-bait rig is difficult because of the
rocks. It is best to straight-line-it with a jig, or
troll with artificial lures.

When the structure to be fished is the edge of a
weed-bed, drop the markers on the outside (Fig.6),
just outside of the weeds as indicated by the depth
finder. If the edge is to be trolled, drop the markers at the first indication of weeds on the inside.
In this situation it is best to troll with a slip sinker
rig. Northern pike frequent the weedline and a
walleye fisherman does not need the aggravation.

Generally speaking, if still-fishing is involved during the day, work from the outside of the structure. During early morning and evening, work
from the shallow side of the structure.

E6   LAKES DURING SUMMER; Summer
      Drift, Trolling and Back-trolling

Drifting is the slowest way of working a
structure. Trolling is the fastest way. And back-
trolling is the most comprehensive way. Each will
be covered thoroughly, because each is important
in its own right. Certain conditions will dictate the
method to be used.

Drifting allows you to cover the structure slowly
if there is little wind; gives you another method to
fish when the wind is too strong; and is the only
way on lakes that are closed to motor-trolling.

Motor trolling allows you to cover large bodies of
water quickly. I won the 1978 National Walleye
Tournament by trolling. I found active fish on different structures, some were over one mile apart.

Back-trolling allows you to fish a structure very
thoroughly. And to cover water efficiently. Boat-
control is the key word. The speed is usually dic-
tated by the method of attack and depth of water
to be fished. All must be taken into consideration.

The type of drifting that is most productive is
not the kind that is associated with a sentimental
slumber, beer in hand and sun-burn as one drifts
across the over-sized water bed. It is a controlled
action created by the turning of the motor and an
occasional start to realign position (Illustration 109
Fig. 1). The motor (not-running) acts as a keel,
helping to keep the boat on course while drifting
broadside along the dropoff. Turning it one way
or the other affects the position of the bow. Once
off course, you must start the outboard (or row)
and move back into positon resuming the controlled drift. Drifting along a shoreline break until fish
are found can be productive. Once fish are located

ILLUSTRATION 109

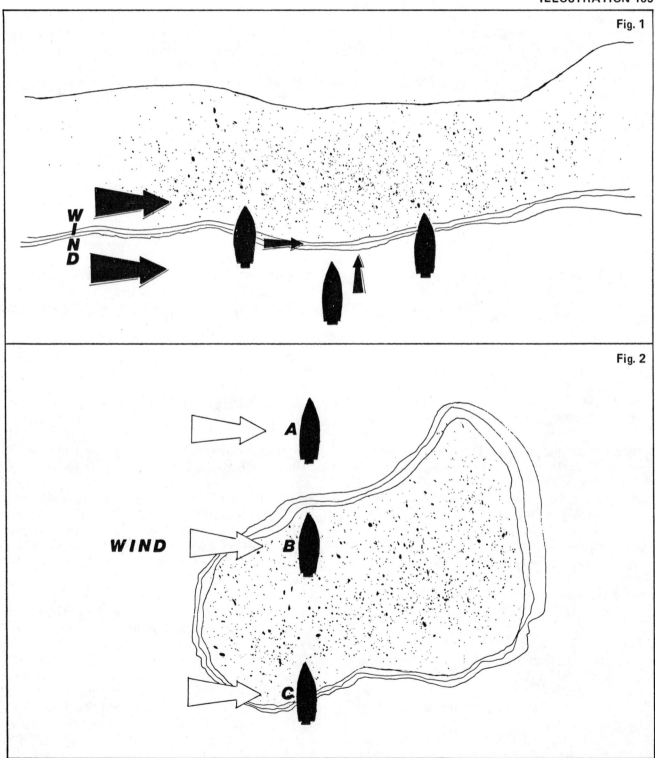

Fig. 1

Fig. 2

it is best to anchor and still-fish the area.

Drifting across under-water bars helps to locate concentrations of walleyes. Drop a marker when a fish is caught and resume the drift. At times you will find two or three hotspots on the bar. Position your boat between them, anchor and still-fish (by cast and retrieve) the bars. If the action stops, drift over the spots again. The drifting of the boat imparts some action to the bait, and this action may be the determining factor. Look at *Fig. (2)*, note that the boat is drifting across the bar at position (A) then (B) and finally (C). In this manner you will cover the bar thoroughly. Note the fish catching positions and work those areas over carefully.

An electric motor is a valuable tool. If you have one, use it to position yourself on the drift. Be careful not to have your line in the water on lakes that do not permit trolling. Use it as a positioning tool and then turn it off and resume your drift.

There are more options open for fishermen who troll than any other method. While trolling one can: troll to drag along the bottom; troll to bounce off the bottom; troll just above the bottom; troll for suspended fish when the opportunity arises; speed troll; slow troll; troll and cast; troll with your outboard; troll with your electric motor or by rowing. If you make sharp turns in and out while trolling, your lure rides high and fast, then drops with each turn enticing a fish that might be chasing the lure.

Every lure that is manufactured has its own optimum point of operating speed to attain a certain depth. Beyond that point, the lure will tend to rise due to water resistance on the line and lure itself. Speed trolling requires certain types of lures. Take the Spoonplug for example, it can be trolled at high speeds without demanding more line and rising, due to resistance. Some of the crankbaits on the market (even though designed for deep water) will rise at a much lower speed.

As speed increases, monofilament line stretches. Over a period of time the line breaks down much quicker than through normal use. But the stretch factor has the ability to accept shock, thereby limiting its hooking potential. It boils down to, using lures that have exceptionally sharp hooks when using monofilament line. There are some lines on the market that stretch very little. They are excellent to use. But if you use a thin diameter line which helps to get the lure down quicker, you may lose a fish due to the shock of striking. And if you use a thick diameter line, you have to have plenty of it to over-come the water resistance.

If you are a full-fledged troller, wire line is the answer. When medium and slow trolling speeds are used or medium depths of water are fished, the monofilament or no-stretch lines are fine, but when speed trolling or deep water trolling, use the wire line. Trolling is a specialized, refined method of fishing that requires the correct tools to get the job done.

To get an idea of how much time should be devoted to various speeds of trolling, it might be broken down this way; speed trolling, 5% of your time; medium speed, 45% of your time and; slow-trolling, 50% of your time. The tables would be turned considerably when fishing for other species, like the northern pike which would require a lot more speed trolling.

The depth of water and type of lure make a great deal of difference. In deep water, troll slowly to stay in contact with the bottom. In medium depths you can troll a bit faster. Some lures have more action than others. A tight-action crankbait can be trolled very slowly to get maximum performance out of the lure. A loose action crankbait must be trolled at a higher rate of speed to attain the same performance. Use the above information when choosing speed and lures. Another thing: when fishing under fair to good conditions, the speed can be increased; under poor conditions troll at a lower speed.

Trolling has become a way of life for more than a few of todays top fishermen. When properly executed, trolling is work, requiring proper lure presentation at the correct depth while maintaining an awareness of the contour to be followed. Run the contour to find out what it looks like, pick out prospective trolling areas (and mark it if you intend to troll over one area repeatedly), then choose your lures according to speed; season; and depth.

Looking at *Illustration 110 Fig.(1)*, run along the break to get a mental picture of it. Then troll a-

ILLUSTRATION 110

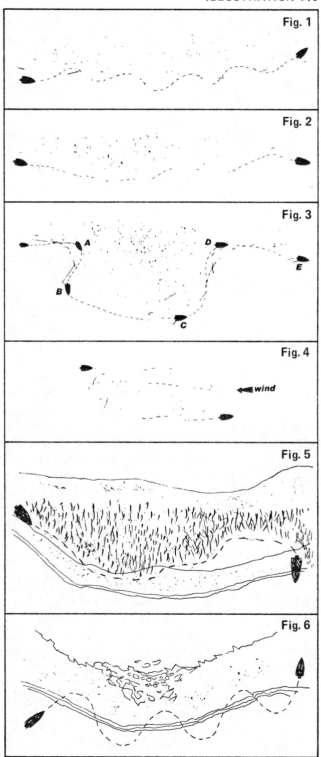

Fig. 1

Fig. 2

Fig. 3

Fig. 4

Fig. 5

Fig. 6

long it, moving in and out slightly. You will accomplish two important things: the lure should bump the side of the break creating an excitement that walleyes like and the lure will change speed and depth as the turns are made. You are looking for a trigger, something to cause a strike.

In *Fig. (2),* run along the outside of the break. Active fish will suspend, and at times are caught off of the break. If working a point *(Fig. 3),* come into the point from (A) travel to the shallow water to get your lure near the edge; turn and travel back out to the break towards (B), swing wide while approaching (C), back down towards (D), move in close enough to keep the lure at the edge, then turn and move out to (E). Now turn around and go back the same way. At times the walleye will take a lure coming from one direction and not another. When trolling on a bar *(Fig. 4)* troll down one side, up the other and then down the middle. Nothing fancy about that. The object is to find fish.

Trolling along a weedbed *(Fig. 5)* presents special problems. The obvious one is entanglement in the weeds. Another is northern pike. They frequent the weedbeds and will readily take a trolled lure. But, there are times that walleyes also inhabit weedbeds and the area below them, so they are important to fishermen. Troll along the outside of the weedbed with bottom bumping lures, and closer with lures that travel a couple of feet off of the bottom.

Cliffs are easy to fish *(Fig. 6)* and treated as two separate pieces of structure. Troll along the top of the break, moving in and out as you go. This will take care of any active fish that may be hanging along the dropoff. Next, troll slowly in the deep water along the first major break. Make sure that you are bottom bumping. The rocks set up a perfect situation for bottom bumping. Lower your lure until you make definite bottom contact *(Fig. 7),* take up a foot or two of line so your lure hits the bottom occasionally. It can create a lot of excitement.

Back-trolling is truly an art, developed by Al and Ron Lindner. It is a method that was created to give the angler boat-control and a precise means of working structure. It was a very important step in

ILLUSTRATION 110

Fig. 7

BUMP BOTTOM

ILLUSTRATION 111

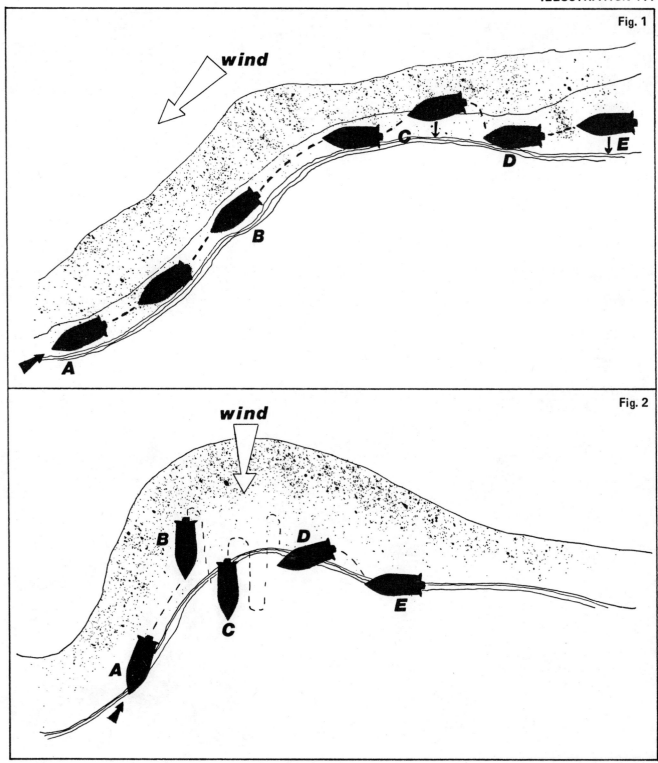

Fig. 1

wind

C

D

E

B

A

Fig. 2

wind

B

D

C

E

A

the development of modern walleye angling. Back-trolling was developed as a means of trolling backwards into the wind, utilizing the motor as a pivot point while manipulating the boat along the structure. The method has maturely evolved to include trolling backwards into the wind; using the wind as a device to hover over structure while the outboard is trolled down to secure a standstill; using the combination of trolling backwards and putting the motor into neutral to let the wind readjust the boat on the structure; using an electric motor (on the transom) to manuver backwards (as a pivot point) along the structure; and as a method to use on perfectly calm days. It doesn't take long to learn how to back-troll. It does take a while to do it effectively. Back-trolling is a method that is live-bait orientated. It can be used to fish for any species.

The object is: (1) to follow the contour as closely as possible; (2) to keep the speed low enough to have bottom contact with your bait, in as short a distance possible. The back-trolling rig itself is discussed in the boat section. You must have a depth finder and a boat and motor set-up that is practical to work with. The baits are discussed later.

Understanding how to maneuver is extremely important. It takes practice because all structures are not straight and the wind is not always on your side. For example, *Illustration 111 Fig. (1)*: troll backwards slowly starting from (A); at (B) start to maneuver towards (C). Now switch it into neutral and drift over the break. Then at (D) put it in reverse and come over the break again. At position (E) drift over the break and continue in this fashion. Your eyes must be glued to the depth finder and have an awareness of the feeling transmitted through the line. Use the motor and wind as a tool to work an area over thoroughly.

The fisherman in *Fig. (2)* will work the corner over fairly well before resuming on his course. In (A) he is backtrolling into position (B), allowing the wind to slide him to (C). He backtrolls back to (B) and slides past position (C) to (D); then resumes his backtrolling and drifting along the drop-off. If he wanted to spend more time, he could have hovered back and forth between (B) and (C) for as long as he wanted to.

ILLUSTRATION 111, Fig. 3

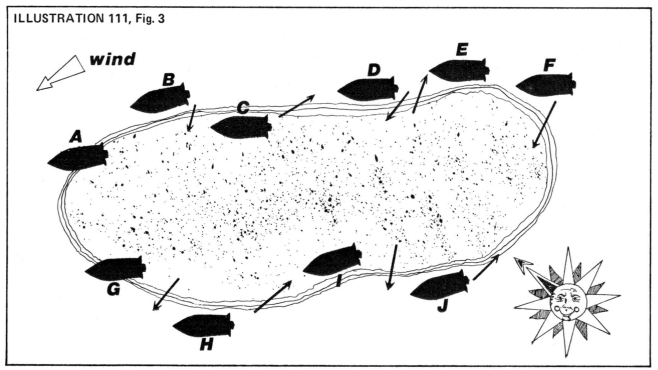

ILLUSTRATION 111

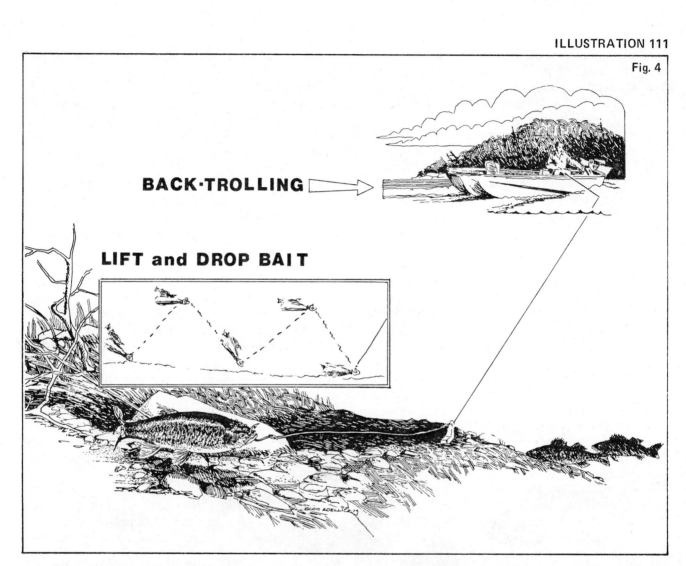

BACK-TROLLING

LIFT and DROP BAIT

Fig. 4

While working a large gravel bar or underwater island *(Fig.3)*, there are a number of ways in which it could be successfully backtrolled. One of those ways is shown. With the sun in the position shown, your attack would be on the shady side of the bar first. Back-troll along the edge from (A) to (B); drift up to position (C); back-troll to position (D); drift in and back-troll to (E); continue to (F) and drift down the edge until you pass the break. Then motor over to (G) and repeat the process. A greater percentage of time would be spent on areas (A) and (F).

The length of line let out will be determined by the depth of water that is to be fished. Generally, in fifteen feet of water or less it is okay to allow a longer line. However, anything over that should be short-lined. The combination of slow trolling speeds and a heavier sinker helps to keep the distance between your rod and the bottom to a minimum. The short line accomplishes two main objectives: you are accurately fishing the structure below, and you will have greater feel for the bottom content and strikes. FOLLOW THE STRUCTURE CLOSELY AND STAY IN CONTACT WITH THE BOTTOM.

As in *Fig. (4)*, a slight lifting and dropping of the bait helps to entice walleyes and helps to feel the bottom. You can actually tell if you're over rocks, which transmits a knocking kind of feeling; over sand, it sort of grabs your bait, feels very sticky or;

over mud that has a drag feel to it. You will learn to recognize the feelings as time goes on.

E7   LAKES DURING SUMMER; Summer
Day or Night

There has been more written about daytime fishing than any other specific time. The reasons are quite obvious and valid. However, the sophisticated angler is looking for new horizons. They want bigger fish quicker or have to make the best of the fishing time that is available to them. Others may find the curiosity of darkness overwhelming, almost daring themselves into trying to fish it. I became one of those individuals, researching fish at night for more than seven years.

My equipment consisted of 200,000 candle power Q-Beam spot lights, a temperature gauge, sampling jars, pad of paper for documentation, bug repellent and often times a face mask to keep out the cool damp air on misty nights. Observing walleyes and other fish in their own environment has taught me a lot about them; most of these lessons are adaptable to their daytime habits.

At first I had pictured the walleyes as being a migratory species moving from deep water into the shallows at night and returning to deep water by morning. I don't agree with that theory anymore. In some lakes they must travel to the shallows at night for food. However, for the most part there is a split. There is a gro'/) of walleyes that spend most of their lives in shallow water, a group that spends most of their lives in extremely deep water (in trout type lakes) and a group that migrates between shallow and deep water. All three of these groups may exist in the same lake, but that is rare. Most lakes have both migratory and shallow water groups which may be determined by: (1) what the food supply is and where it is, (2) the amount of predators present and (3) the amount of deeper water that is available.

Generally speaking, if a lake has a lot of weeds in it along the shoreline, you will probably find a population of shallow water walleyes that live in those weeds. At night when conditions are right, they will prowl through the weeds feeding heavily. These fish are virtually untouched by fishing pressure and some are very big. They are in very loose groups and show up night after night. The migratory walleye will move up to the shallows when conditions are right and prowl throughout gravel, rock and sand areas.

There is a very logical explanation for the shallow walleye. The weeds are chocked full of food. There are minnows, larvae, and more. The base of the weeds is usually cool even during a hot summer. And the weeds offer an unlimited amount of cover. The following experience may help you in understanding the walleye:

I had been conducting some research on a lake in central Wisconsin.

The conditions were right, and I spotted many walleyes. Most were small, averaging about two pounds. The water was clear and my 200,00 candle power spot-light penetrated deep. But tonight my objective was to shine the weeds for large fish.

When looking over a long distance the smaller walleyes eyes shined bright looking like marbles; the larger walleyes eyes had a yellow-orange tint to them and were the size of quarters and some cases half-dollars. I spotted a few, but not as many as expected.

Suddenly, large half-dollar size headlights were seen towards shore, a sparse weed area. It didn't take long to reach her. The walleye moved along slowly as if it didn't care whether I was there or not. Then it quickened its pace and disappeared. I was a long ways from the dropoff and gave pursuit. Moving along slowly, I had seen a bit of white; it was the lower portion of her tail.

Here she lay, her head was buried under some weeds and her long thirty inch or better body laid right out in the open. Obviously it felt secure (like an ostrich). I brushed the oar against her and she wiggled to keep her head under the weed. I left her there.

I have witnessed this behavior a number of times over the years. The walleye can make use of the weeds for cover, and it is difficult to see them even when looking right at them. Some fish have very distinct markings on them and appear in the same areas night after night. While instructing at Al Lindner's In' Fisherman Schools, I observed one walleye on Gull Lake, Minnesota, two years in a row, inhabiting the same area. It had an unusual round spot on its back. The fish weighed nine lbs.

I believe that these shallow water fish live in the weeds until the food thins out, then move a little deeper or find new areas of the shallows. It is not a migratory fish by any means, nor a schooling fish. A good food shelf may draw a few fish to the area because of the fact that it is a good food shelf. The number of fish in the shallows will increase when other deep water walleyes migrate to the shallows during the shallow water periods. This would be during spawning and late fall most noticeably, and the shallow water period of early summer. The kind of weed present hardly makes a difference. The common denominator is food. During the day they are very difficult to catch, and at night, when conditions are right, they are vulnerable, taking live-bait as well as artificial bait from cautious fishermen.

On the other hand, some lakes have the migratory walleye that spends a great deal of time in transit. The cover of expansive weed beds aren't present, so the fish that move up at night, move back down to deeper waters during the day. They have a schooling nature and are found in common areas where we as fishermen have been used to catching them.

The deeper water walleye is common in trout lakes that have an abundance of suspended forage and plenty of oxygen in deeper waters. These walleyes (like all of the other types), follow the movements of the suspended forage.

All of the walleyes mentioned are of the same specie, take on the general color tones of their environment and can change their patterns or life styles. The most important point to remember is: Walleyes follow their food and live in proximity to it! For them, it's the "law of survival".

I have mentioned the term "conditions" several times. Just as there are favorable conditions during the day, at night there are conditions that are good or bad. The conclusions of what conditions are good and which are bad have been well pinpointed during my seven years of night research. Here's what I found:

NO MOON; This has been a favorable condition. Walleyes are active, and a lot of fish have been observed in the shallow water.

THIRD-QUARTER MOON; A favorable condition, much activity, although not as much as during a no moon stage.

FIRST-QUARTER MOON; Nights are bright and get brighter as a full moon sets in. Walleyes not as active, and there are fewer of them in the shallows.

FULL MOON; I haven't observed many walleyes occupying shallow water. The ones observed seemed spooky. I have not caught many fish in the shallows unless fishing in the shadows cast by trees and other land objects (occasionally the moon will cast shadows along the shoreline).

LOW-PRESSURE SYSTEM; Much shallow water activity, fish seem easier to catch.

A CHANGE TO A LOW-PRESSURE SYSTEM; Favorable condition, observed a lot of fish and they were easy to catch.

A CHANGE TO A HIGH-PRESSURE SYSTEM; Walleyes were a bit spooky, not as many observed in the shallows and they seemed reluctant to strike.

A HIGH-PRESSURE SYSTEM; The walleyes were spooky, reluctant to strike, and there were fewer fish in the shallows.

CALM WATER, LIKE GLASS; On the side of the lake that is calm, walleyes move very shallow and appear to be active.

RIPPLE ON THE WATER; Favorable condition, but walleyes are reluctant to move to extreme shallows. Best fishing in a little deeper water (possibly four feet of water or deeper).

WHITE-CAPS; I haven't observed walleyes in super-shallow water. Most successful fish catching done in six or more feet of water.

STORM — THUNDER, LIGHTNING; I haven't observed active walleyes in shallow water. Best thing is to forget fishing under these conditions.

CLOUDY NIGHT; A favorable condition, observed many walleyes and have caught decent fish. When dense cloud cover is present under a full moon, the condition turns for the better. The fish seem to become active, as where a full moon is a bad condition.

PARTLY CLOUDY; When associated with other good conditions, the walleyes were active and shallow. When associated with bad conditions they

ILLUSTRATION 200

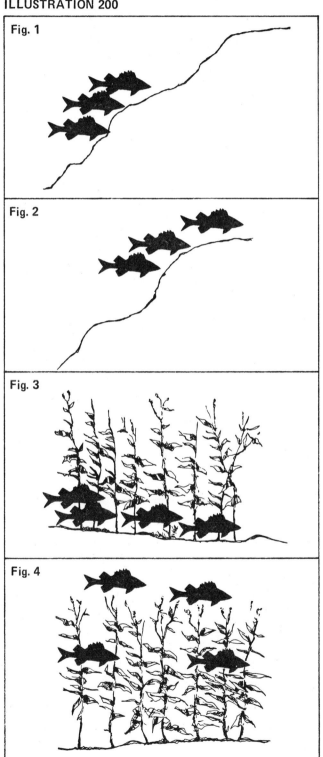

Fig. 1

Fig. 2

Fig. 3

Fig. 4

were spooky and reluctant to hit.

CLEAR NIGHT; Generally associated with a high-pressure system. Not the best condition. Walleyes seemed a bit spooky. Better fishing in deeper water.

BRIGHT NIGHT; You can almost see shadows cast by trees along the shoreline. The moon is not out, but the night is very bright. The stars seem to gleam, and occasionally there is an "aurora borealis" present. It is usually associated with a high pressure system. Walleyes are not as abundantly seen, and fishing is tough. The best thing to do is fish along the break, rather than the shallows.

HUMIDITY; Baitfish tend to rise off the bottom when the humidity is high. Walleyes that are searching for food suspend and prowl over the tops of the weeds in shallow water. If associated with other favorable conditions, it's a bonanza!

When all of the good conditions apply to the night at hand, fishing for walleye is a cinch. It's time to fish for that wall-hanger. Because of the fact that it is untapped you have a good chance of landing a big fish. They are there!

Movement into the shallows takes place quite early in the evening in most lakes. The exception is in clear water lakes. Usually movement into the shallows on clear bodies of water, takes place much later at night. Also, the greater amount of activity on the lake, the later they move.

The migratory walleye *(illustration 200 Fig. 1 & 2)* usually holds it position just off the dropoff *(Fig. 1)* during the day, and moves into the shallows *(Fig. 2)* at night.

The weed walleye holds in the deeper weeds *(Fig. 3)* during the day and moves into the shallower weeds *(Fig. 4)* at night.

The greatest percentage of walleyes in all of the cases will not move all the way in, just a small percentage of the actual group moves in super shallow.

Fishing in the weeds at night is tough. I have developed a couple of methods that work very well. One method is "Skimming". Skimming is working the small amount of water that is between the tops of the weeds and the surface *(illustration 201 Fig. 1)*. I like to use an electric motor when skimming. An outboard can be used, but it must be trolled down to a crawl. Both artificial lures and live baits are effective in the art of skimming.

The choice of artificial lure is important. It must have exceptionally sharp hooks and be a shallow-running floater. Examples are: The Floating Rapala; the Jointed Rapala; the Floating Rebel and the Jointed Rebel; Cotton Cordell's Red Fin or other imitation minnow types that don't dive deep upon retrieves and float at rest. The reel should be equipped with eight or ten pound test line and have capabilities of holding about two-hundred yards of line.

Trolling over walleyes in shallow water doesn't seem to bother them unless you change speeds. The slightest change in sound created by changing speed spooks them. A steady sound may move them a bit, but they will return within seconds. This is one of the reasons for long-lining it. Get that line out there a good fifty yards or better. Trolling a floater at a crawl, with fifty yards of line out means a long bow *(illustration 201 Fig. 2)* in your line. The bow won't hamper your success if you have extremely sharp hooks. Hold your rod high, every little while lift the rod higher, to about 12:00 o'clock position. This adds a little speed to

the lure and allows it to dive skimming the tops of the weeds. Then resume the 3:00 o'clock position. This movement helps to entice the walleye. It gives the walleye a chance to calculate an attack. This method works best in water that is less than eight feet deep. If you are confident that big fish are working an area, skim back and forth a few times. The walleyes are there, although not active at all times. Fish the same areas often. Don't give up just because you did not catch a fish the first time.

There is another artificial method that I had used for bass fishing but did not realize its potential for walleyes at night. A friend of mine, Roy Sherock (of Milwaukee, Wisc.) brought it to my attention. Roy had been night fishing for some time now. He has taken some very nice catches of bass and walleye. The fish had come from lakes near large cities which had a lot of fishing pressure. He was using "spinner-baits". Most were single-spins and Roy had a lot of confidence in black. After trying it several times, I found that as long as the color of the spinner-bait was dark, it didn't make much difference as to actual color.

ILLUSTRATION 201, Fig. 1

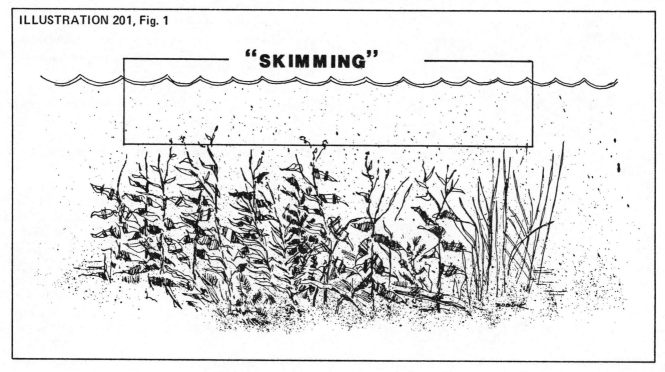

"SKIMMING"

The weed walleye and migratory walleye seemed to take the spinner quite well. A similar spinner is used for catching suspended walleye on Lake Erie. A steady retrieve with an occasional drop seemed to work best. Since using this method I have taken several fish over five pounds, along with many small walleyes. This was over a three month period of trying the method. I have also found that a trailer hook is almost a necessity. The method has worked over weeds and areas of the shoreline that had a dropoff nearby. Roy has caught many bass over four pounds while fishing with this method.

The best way to maneuver around the shallows is with an electric trolling motor. Position the boat near the edge of the weeds and continue working in until you have covered the shoreline quite thoroughly, then move on to another weedbed. Eight or ten pound line is sufficient.

Skimming with live-bait can be very productive. I have found an excellent rig for skimming with live-bait. It has a couple of red beads and a small spinner blade on the snell just ahead of a number eight or ten hook. If working the shallow weeds, don't use a sinker. If working deeper weeds use a very small split-shot sinker about twelve inches a-

bove the hook. Occasionally I will use two hooks in tandem. The second hook is secured behind the first with a piece of monofilament line. The rig is best used with a nightcrawler, although leeches and minnows will work. The same slow troll and bow-in-line method of skimming applies. Try to tick the tops of the weeds, occasionally it will trigger a strike. This method has been responsible for many fish over two pounds being landed. A friend, who is a big-fish fisherman, Brad Miller, has done very well catching his share of big walleye by using these methods.

Other methods of catching walleye at night include casting along the shallows with Rapalas and tight-action crank-baits; trolling crank-baits along the dropoff; and hovering over the break casting a jig and minnow combination toward the shallows and retrieving them down the break.

While fishing at night, use as little light as is legally possible. The light is nice for crappies and it doesn't seem to bother the bass that much, but walleyes like it dark. Your fishing success will improve with the minimum amount of light. During the day, fish in proximity to areas that have been productive night fishing spots.

ILLUSTRATION 201, Fig. 2

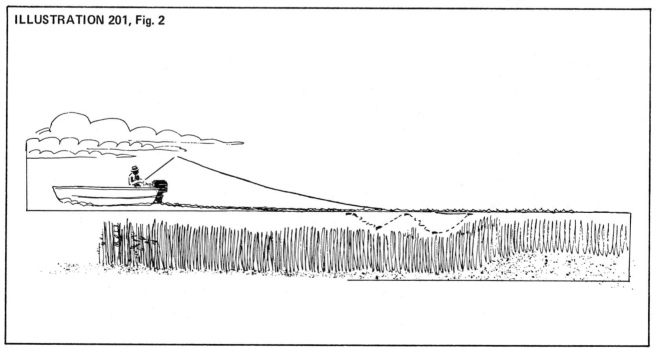

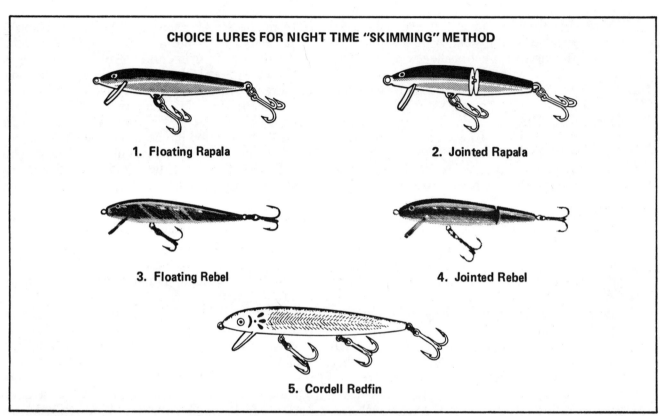

CHOICE LURES FOR NIGHT TIME "SKIMMING" METHOD

1. Floating Rapala

2. Jointed Rapala

3. Floating Rebel

4. Jointed Rebel

5. Cordell Redfin

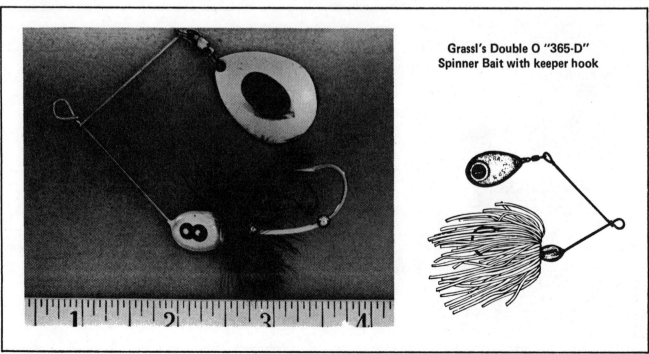

Grassl's Double O "365-D"
Spinner Bait with keeper hook

E8   LAKES DURING SUMMER; Summer
        Successful Artificial Lures

To recap the time period: the migratory wall-eyes are schooled in mid to shallow depths and the weed walleyes are in an active stage (mostly at night). The choice of artificial lures will be determined by the depth in which there is fish activity. This means some experimenting on your part.

Some artificials are designed to work at any depth. An example would be a jig. Others have

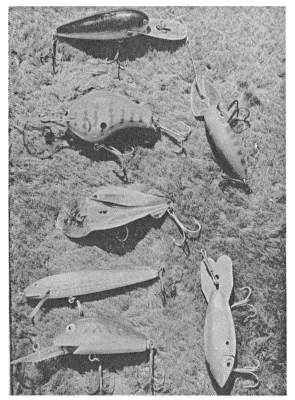

LURES for different depths: Rapala Fatrap, Bagley Balsa B, Cisco Kid, Spoonplug, Rebel Minnow & Deep Diver, Bomber

been designed to run at certain depths. There are tight-action crank-baits and loose-action crank-baits (previously discussed). Then in basic design, there are fat, almost round types and long narrow types of plugs. Generally, walleyes prefer the tight-action, long narrow baits over the short, loose-action crank-baits. There are exceptions like the Spoonplug which attracts more than its share of walleyes. You want as many things in your

favor as possible, so use high percentage lures.

The size of the artificial bait is also important. For numbers of fish follow this simple chart:

EARLY SPRING UNTIL MID-SUMMER	SMALL LURES
MID-SUMMER UNTIL FIRST FROST	MEDIUM SIZE
FIRST FROST UNTIL FREEZE UP	SMALL AND VERY LARGE
FREEZE UP UNTIL THAW	MEDIUM TO LARGE

If you are strictly a big-fish fisherman, use medium to very large size artificial lures all of the time. "Big bait, big fish" is not necessarily the rule, but it does improve your chances of catching trophies.

Rate of speed and retrieve is another important factor in catching fish. For a higher percentage of productivity follow these general guidelines:

EARLY SPRING UNTIL MID-SUMMER	SLOW TO MEDIUM SPEEDS
MID-SUMMER UNTIL LATE SUMMER	SLOW, MEDIUM OR FAST
LATE SUMMER UNTIL FREEZE UP	SLOW, AND SLOW TO MEDIUM
FREEZE UP UNTIL SPAWN	SLOW TO MEDIUM
A MAJOR CHANGE OF WEATHER	VERY SLOW
POOR CONDITIONS	VERY SLOW
GOOD CONDITIONS	SLOW, MEDIUM OR FAST (DEPENDING ON CONDITION)
AT NIGHT	SLOW TO FAST
TIGHT-ACTION CRANK-BAITS	SLOW TO MEDIUM
LOOSE-ACTION CRANK-BAITS	MEDIUM TO FAST

Often times the speed of retrieve and depth of water fished are in direct relationship to each other. In shallow water, it would be easy to attain slow, medium and fast retrieves. At medium depths, the same would apply, but fast retrieves mean a narrower choice of lures available. In deep water, slow to medium retrieves are readily attained, but the choice of lures for fast retrieves is narrowed down to just a few. So weight must be added to smaller lures.

The question most fishermen don't like asking is: "Should I use a snap swivel with artificial lures or not?" A snap swivel helps to prevent line twist and is convenient when a number of lure changes are desired. The snap swivel has its time and place. When fast fishing, I will use a snap swivel whenever possible. When slow fishing, I won't use it. "Fast fishing" is trolling, or using fast retrieves, where the fish does not have time to examine the lure; you're working on the fishes strike instinct. "Slow fishing" is fishing at a very slow pace. The fish can visually look the bait over before attacking. This is

working on its hunger instincts. Tying a knot directly to a lure, restricts its action. So if I want to restrict the action of a loose-action crank-bait to make the action tighter (a plus when walleye fishing), I'll tie a knot instead of using a snap swivel. The color of the snap swivel can make a little difference. In order of use, this is my choice: (1) a black snap swivel; (2) a brass snap swivel and (3) a silver snap swivel.

When using straight line spinner baits (like a Mepps), use a black snap swivel. When using a safety-pin-type spinner bait, don't use a snap swivel. Don't use the snap on a hair-pin-type spinner bait because it seems to foul the bait up frequently.

Adding a split-shot sinker for weight (just ahead of the bait) does not seem to make much difference when using crank-baits. Several split-shots do impair action, however. Instead, go to a larger sinker.

While setting up your tackle box for walleye fishing remember that depth of water to be covered is of prime importance. As far as artificial baits go, you should have some of the following:

1. JIGS 1/8,1/4,3/8,1/2
   5/8 and 3/4 ounce
2. TIGHT ACTION CRANK-BAITS . . . . . .
   to run 0' to 6' deep
   to run between 6' and 12'
   to run between 10' and 18'
   to run between 15' and 25'
3. MINNOW IMITATION LURES . . . .
   several 3', 5' and 7' sizes
4. SPOONPLUGS . . . . . to cover all depths
5. SPINNER-BAITS . . . .
   just a couple of single spins
6. LARGE CRANK-BAITS . . just a couple
7. SNAP SWIVELS . . . . plenty of black
8. STINGER HOOKS . . . . . . extra hooks
   for the spinner-bait and jigs
9. PLASTIC BODY GRUBS . . . .
   1/8 to 3/8 ounce
10. NAIL CLIPPERS . . . . a must

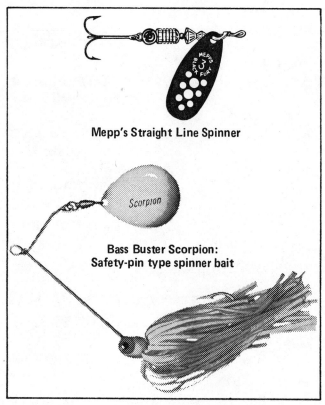

Mepp's Straight Line Spinner

Bass Buster Scorpion:
Safety-pin type spinner bait

Use the process of elimination starting with time of year; type of lake; clarity of water; information from the natives; main food sources and pursue the lake accordingly. Troll in various depths of water. After locating some fish, keep the depth in mind. Work with the artificials that are designed to run at those depths, or move on to live-bait methods.

E9   LAKES DURING SUMMER; Summer Live-Bait Methods

Most of the live-bait methods will adapt for use during any open water time of the year. Getting acquainted with the tools and their workings is essential. Each of them has been designed with a purpose in mind, filling a gap as a productive means to catch fish. All too often, fishermen get hooked to a method of catching fish and never change, even when the situation calls for other tactics. Adaptability separates the good fisherman from the mediocre one. Adapting to unfamiliar methods is not an easy task. The time to try

new methods is when you are catching fish to make sure that they work. Then try them when you're not catching fish.

There are rigs that are available through most of the sport shops and others are home-made, using the same basic components as their commercial counterparts. Both the rigs and components are explained.

The components of the live-bait rigs consist of various members of the terminal-tackle family. The variations are unlimited. Included with the paraphernalia are suggestions as to its uses. *Illustration 202, Fig. (1)* shows the Removable Split-Shot. It is the most practical split-shot on the market. When working deeper water, simply add some shot to your line. When working shallow, remove the split-shot by pinching the back-side. You will save money because it can be removed from the line. The Removable Split-Shot works well with a simple bobber, snell and shot combination.

Slip Shot, *Fig. (2):* The slip shot has a hole in it. It can slide down the line to a stopper (usually a

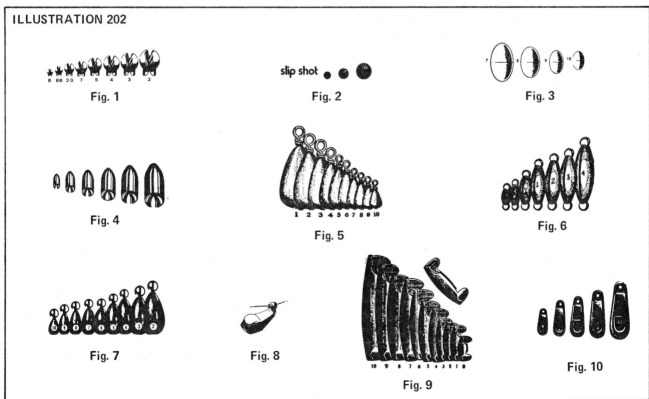

ILLUSTRATION 202

Fig. 1

slip shot

Fig. 2

Fig. 3

Fig. 4

Fig. 5

Fig. 6

Fig. 7

Fig. 8

Fig. 9

Fig. 10

barrel swivel, *Illustration 203, Fig. 12)*. It is best used in shallow water, where lighter weights are used. Occasionally the slip-shot is inserted into the minnows mouth, forcing it into its stomach with a pen or pencil. This adds weight to the minnow and frees the line from weed catching sinkers. It is used in this manner when using a dead minnow in place of an artificial one.

Egg Sinkers *Fig. (3):* The egg sinker has a hole going through the center. Several can be attached to the line for trolling situations. Its shape helps to keep it from catching in the rocks.

Bullet Sinkers *Fig. (4):* The bullet sinker is a sliding sinker and primarily used for a plastic worm fishing for largemouth bass. But it can be used with a live nightcrawler when fishing for walleye. The open end of the bullet sinker slides down to the hook. Occasionally an angler will insert the tip of a toothpick into the bullet end, this keeps it in place. Light weight bullet sinkers are used.

Bell Sinker *Fig.(5):* The bell sinker is an old reliable, used for many years in all parts of the coun-

try. In some areas it is known as the "drop sinker"; so called because it is usually hung on the end of the line while hooks are suspended above it. The sinker rests on the bottom and works best in current. The original "Wolf River Rig" consists of the bell sinker, a three way swivel *(Fig. 11),* and snell.

Rubbercore Sinker, *Fig. (6):* This sinker is particularly nice to use. A simple twist of the line around the rubber core is all that is needed to apply it to the line. A fisherman can add or take weights off quickly. It is used for trolling, casting, or still-fishing.

Snap Loc™ Dipsey Swivel Sinker, *Fig. (7):* Water Gremlin's come up with a new bell shaped sliding sinker. It won't cause any line damage because of its easy installation. Simply slip the line through its celcon eye and you're all set to go. Use it for bottom bumping and trolling. The heavier ones can be used to free-up lures that might have gotten snagged.

Mister Twister Interchangeable Eyelet Sinker,

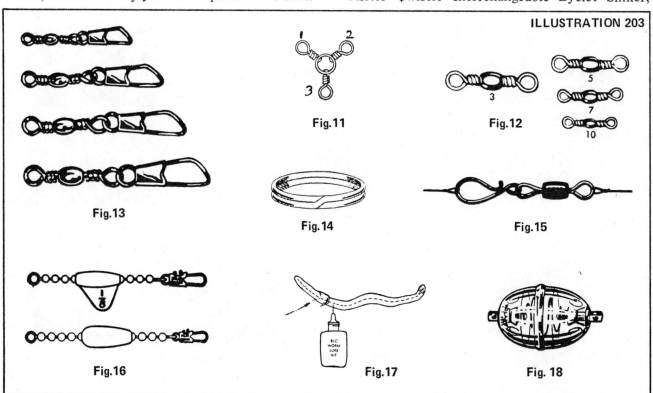

ILLUSTRATION 203

Fig. 11

Fig. 12

Fig. 13

Fig. 14

Fig. 15

Fig. 16

Fig. 17

Fig. 18

Fig. (8): The Twister sliding sinker comes with a short plastic tube. The tube serves as protection against line damage that could be caused by the lead. With tube on the line, the open end of the sinker is wrapped (with your fingers) around the tube. The end result is a sliding sinker that will detach when snagged without losing your entire rig (and valuable time re-rigging).

Pinch-On Sinkers, *Fig. (9):* The pinch-on sinker is attached to the line by folding the ears over the line and lightly pressing the body. This sinker is best used with an abrasive-resistant line. Speed trollers like to use this type of sinker because of its ability to hold its position on the line. Trollers that use wire line like the durable pinch-on sinker also.

Lindy's Walking Slip Sinker, *Fig. (10):* This is the original walking sinker that Al and Ron Lindner designed and used so successfully. The hole in the sinker allows free flowing line. This is important when teasing a walleye. As the sinker lays on the bottom, the walleye pulls the bait at the end of the line and does not feel the sinker weight. The bait feels more natural. It can be used during any fishing situation while pursuing the walleye.

Three-Way Swivel, *Illustration 203 Fig. (11):* Besides being the most important component part of the "Wolf-River Rig", it s uses are favored by the trolling clan. The line from the rod is attached to terminal number two; the sinker is attached by a leader to terminal number three, usually a lighter pound test line so if you get hung up the sinker may be lost and the rest of the rig saved; a long snell is attached to terminal number one, it might have a live-bait or an artificial lure attached.

Barrel Swivel, *Fig.(12):* The barrel swivel is a device that is used for attaching one line and another while providing a means of controlling line twist. It also is used as a stopper, keeping the sinker away from the hook. It is a basic component part that should be in every fishermans tackle box.

Snap Swivel, *Fig. (13):* The snap swivel is used as a quick-change tool while keeping line twist to a minimum. It is seldom used while slow fishing, more often used while artificial bait fishing. The snap allows freedom of the lure and does not restrict its action. Sometimes, it is used in place of

a barrel swivel, giving the fisherman an opportunity to change live-bait rigs quickly.

Split Rings, *Fig. (14):* Its most practical use is in attaching hooks to an artificial bait, however, another great use is to tie the end of the line to the split-ring and attach the split-ring to the artificial lure. This enables freedom of action.

Lindy Swivel Clip, *Fig. (15):* A basic component part of the Lindy Rig. Slip the looped end of the snell over the clip, add live-bait and you are all set. Changing snells is easy, and the swivel clip acts as a sliding sinker stopper.

Bead Chain Keel Lead and Trolling Lead, *Fig. (16):* Available in many different weights, the Keel and Trolling Lead are primarily used by fishermen that spend a great deal of time trolling. The Keel Lead cuts the water a bit better and helps to over-come line twist. It is usually used in deeper water where as the Trolling lead is better for flat lines (trolling closer to the surface).

Worm Blower, *Fig. (17):* The worm blower consists of a plastic tube or bottle (empty) and hypodermic needle. Insert the needle into an area just below the sex-band of the nightcrawler. Squeeze the bottle to force air into the nightcrawler. This keeps the nightcrawler just off the bottom and makes it active. The nightcrawler will squirm and twist around . . . hopefully in full view of the walleye.

Water Fillable Slip Bobber, *Fig. (18):* Add weight to the bobber by pushing in one end, allowing it to partially fill with water. The fisherman can control depth or speed of descent. It is great for working over weeds or other obstructions.

The Lindy Rig, *Illustration 204, Fig. (19):* This rig has created a lot of excitement in the world of walleye fishing. The sinker slides down to the swivel clip which is usually a foot or more from the hook. When a walleye strickes allow it to take line. Then reel in your slack line and set the hook. The different size sinkers allow you to work in any depth.

Flikker Rig, *Fig. (20):* Lindy also manufactures the Flikker Rig, which is the same as the Lindy Rig except that it has an attractor. The small blade turns as the rig is retrieved, the beads help to keep the blade in place above the hook. The Flikker

Rig is best used under conditions where current is involved or in darker waters.

Gapen's Bait Walker Snell Rig, *Fig.(21):* This is an excellent snell with an attractor. The beads and willow leaf blade attracts walleyes best when trolled or used in water with current. Personally, I like a smaller hook, so I cut the larger hook off and put on a number eight or ten hook. The willow leaf blade does not rise as fast as a colorado blade, so it is easier to maintain bottom contact.

Mister Twister, Al's Yarn Rig, *Fig. (22):* There's a small piece of yarn attached at the hook. It acts as an added attractor and works very well. When a minnow is attached, it looks as if the minnow is carrying some food in its mouth. The yarn is available in different colors.

Mister Twister Floater Rig, *Fig.(23):* The floating jig keeps the bait off of the bottom. At times walleyes will suspend off the bottom, especially when feeding heavily. This rig can be used with a leech, minnow, or nightcrawler. The sinker is a sliding weight, and can be attached to the line

without cutting it. The floating jig is available in different colors.

Gapen's Bait-Walker with Snell, *Fig. (24):* The Bait-Walker is available with a snell attached. However, this line-drawing shows other possibilities. The line from the rod is attached directly to the hook with Bait-Walker in between. A small split-shot acts as a sinker stopper. This enables the fisherman the ability to slide the split-shot up or down to adjust the length of the snell.

Forward trolling in medium to deep water has always been a problem for the live-bait fisherman. Usually he resorts to a lot of lead on the line or a "Wolf-River-Rig" type of setup. An innovation was needed and it arrived. Dan Gapen, a lure manufacturer from Minnesota, developed the Bait-Walker, a sinker-rig that "fills-the-bill" for the trolling fisherman. It is available from 1/4 to 6 ounces; wide enough of a range for both the shallow water and deep water fishermen. They have become popular on Lake Erie, Lake Winnebago and Mille Lacs where trolling is a way of life for walleye fisher-

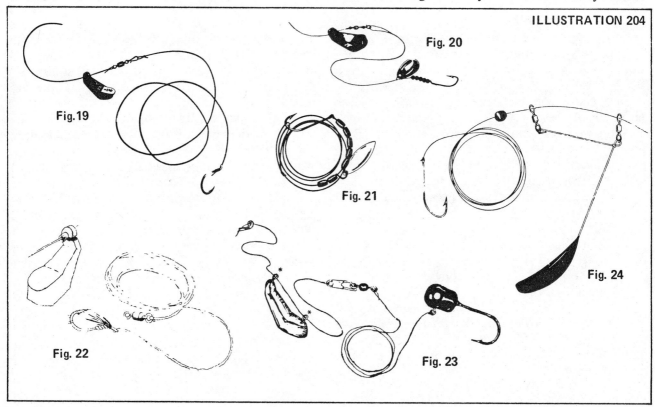

ILLUSTRATION 204

Fig. 19

Fig. 20

Fig. 21

Fig. 22

Fig. 23

Fig. 24

ILLUSTRATION 205

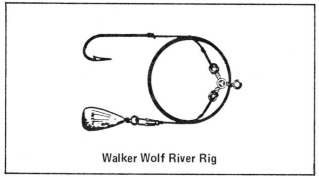

Walker Wolf River Rig

Gapen's

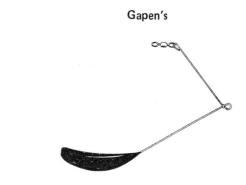

Fig. 1   Bait Walker Sinker

men. The Bait-Walker is composed of a sinker, hair-pin wire and barrel swivel *(illustration 205, Fig.1)*. With sinker alone a fisherman can make up his own rigs or get the Bait-Walker "Live-Bait Snell" *(Fig.2)*. Use it with a leech, nightcrawler, minnow, salamander, or frog. The Bait-walker "Float Rig" *(Fig. 3)* is adjustable and allows the fisherman a choice of trolling depths (although slight) or the option of still-fishing with the rig. In certain situations, particularly in current, a "Floating Jig Head" *(Fig. 4)* helps to keep the bait up off the rocks. An excellent rig for trolling very slowly. In some areas they call it a "poor-mans down-rigger". When adding my own snell I will use a thirty-six inch piece of monofilament and number eight to ten bait hook and make my adaptions from there. We are fishing for active fish and the weight doesn't seem to bother them.

Fig. 2   Bait Walker "live bait snell"

F1   LAKES DURING SUMMER; Post-Summer
The Journey to Deep Water

The summer slowly progresses to a peak. Walleye fishing starts to taper off. The fifteen and eighteen foot flats that were productive now dry up. All of this seems to happen at a time when the fisherman feels that he has mastered the art of walleye fishing. In the northern part of the country this usually takes place during mid-July; in the mid-section, near the end of June; and southern portions, around mid-June. The walleyes have taken the journey to deep water.

The shallow water walleyes move into the weeds, making them tough to catch during the day, unless you have sparse weed situations. The migratory walleyes (still schooled) make their way towards

Bait Float →

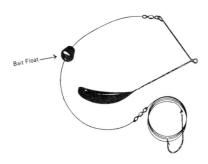

Fig. 3   Bait Walker "float rig"

Fig. 4   Bait Walker "floating jig head"

deeper water. There are a number of reasons that may explain their actions.

Bait-fish start heading for deeper water. Crappies will suspend over deep water and bluegills move to deeper water. The perch that are the young-of-the-year split up. Some move to deep water along with the larger perch and some occupy the weed areas. Some lakes have ample oxygen levels in deeper water, enough to sustain the walleyes needs.

Of the bait-fish and walleyes that are caught during this time, some have various types of aquatic insects in their stomachs. There is a shift in the food supply with panfish moving deep. A portion of their diet consists of aquatic insects and larva. The result: a great percentage of the walleye population moves to the deep water MUD FLATS and other deep water structure that draw baitfish and aquatic creatures. Others suspend.

Fishermen are starting to fish the harder mud flats in deep water (forty, fifty and sixty) and coming up with good fish. Every now and then a fisherman will run across a group of large fish. They are schooled tight and seem to be quite brave under the cover-of-the-darkness in deep water. The most productive fishing is done in lakes that do not contain a large population of suspended forage. Typically they are lakes that have a greater percentage of deep water than shallow water and sufficient oxygen. This period usually lasts until there is a depletion of oxygen in the deep water which forces fish to move to shallower water again. It doesn't happen on all lakes, but on lakes that it does, there is another walleye bonanza before the turnover period. The post-summer walleye bonanza *doesn't* seem to happen on the lakes that have these attributes: deep, clear, trout inhabited lakes with a substantial suspended fish population. As you can see, the walleye reacts to the forces of nature with in its environment. Changing lakes to compensate for abnormalities in the behavior patterns can save the day.

The shallow water walleye (if it exists on the lake you are fishing) moves into the weeds and other heavy obstructions. It becomes very active at night when the cover of darkness provides shelter for hunting. During the day it digs in tight and is very difficult to catch. It is best to fish the edge of the weedline both on the inside and outside.

Pay greater attention to the area where the weeds thin out towards deeper water, and the weed clumps *(illustration 206)*. The shoreside of the weeds (A) can be fished with a jig and minnow effectively by snapping the jig through the inner edges of the weeds. The weed clumps (B) can be fished with: crankbaits ticking the weed-tops; a jig and minnow snapped through them; a simple hook, line and bobber setup still-fished; or back-trolled slowly with floating jigs.

F2   LAKES DURING SUMMER; Post-Summer Deep Water Fishing

Deep water fishing during post-summer conditions is tough. A walleye that is in deep water is equivalent to a walleye at night. In most cases, it is very dark and gloomy in forty and fifty foot depths. Smell and sound play an important part. Because of the vast expanses of deep water, schools are often hard to find. Once located, fishing is usually quick until the easy fish are taken. The reluctant fish are much harder to entice.

Look for hard bottom areas. They are made up of gravel, sand, rock or other forms of obstructions. The hard mud areas adjacent to structures should be fished also. Some of the hard mud areas may not be near any vertical type structure. So experimentation is the only way to find them. These areas have not been fished very hard because fishermen have been taught to relate to "obvious structure". In some lakes, the bottom resembles sand dunes, providing many hills and pockets harboring a lot of aquatic insects that draw baitfish and walleye. The walleye can live anyplace that the baitfish can live. So don't be frightened off by depths of fifty or sixty feet if the situation calls for it.

Some lakes are loaded with sheepshead which uproot the bottom a bit while feeding. Often times the walleye follow the sheepshead around feeding on tidbits uprooted by the sheepshead. Most of the native fishermen will stay in an area where they catch sheepshead because they know that the walleye are present. The same goes for white bass. Usually one can catch some walleye near schools of

ILLUSTRATION 206

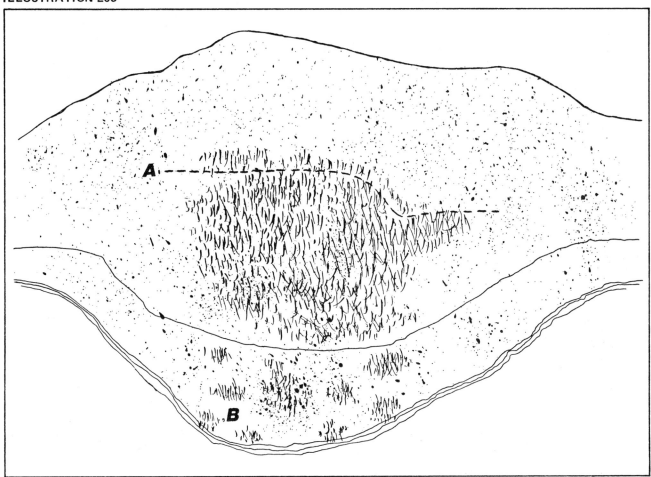

white bass, or just under them. Perch in deep water are a good indication of the presence of gamefish. Find out what is in the perches stomach. If there are a lot of aquatic insects they may be relating to a deep water mud flat that harbors them. Commercial fishermen (when fishing for perch) look for sand. Learn to recognize the signs that tell you whether there's the possibility of the presence of walleye.

Drifting is a good way to present live bait to the walleye. But it is slow and time might win the battle. However, if a school is spread out, you can accomplish a lot by drifting. At this time of the year, drifting with large live bait helps to put you in contact with some very large fish. Use a large golden shiner; five or six inch chub; crayfish, salamander; large leech; or inflated (the pick of the lit-

ter) nightcrawler. A Lindy or Twister Rig will serve as a basic rig for drifting. I like to use a 1/2 ounce or larger sinker to get down to the deeper water. When using a larger sinker, use a longer snell to keep the sinker and bait approximately thirty six inches apart. Should I feel a light pickup by a walleye, I will continue to work the area searching for active fish.

When locating walleyes, drop a marker buoy over the side, and work around it. A tight school may occupy a small amount of space. Precision in locating is important. There is nothing more frustrating than losing a school of fish because you have drifted off your spot. Putting an X on the water doesn't work! Use marker buoys.

The advent of the Bait-Walker makes trolling in deep water a lot easier and more productive than ever before *(Section II, E9)*. With the Bait-Walker Sinker you have a choice of sinker weights ranging from 1/4 ounce to 6 ounces. They will do the job in almost any depth of water. They are designed to get your lure or live bait down to any depth that the walleyes may be in. I am greatly impressed with these products. For working forty and fifty foot depths, you might choose the 3-1/2 ounce size and tie on a lure that extends three or four feet behind the Bait-Walker. Forward troll along the base of vertical structures and across the mud flats. Choose imitation-minnow-type lures or tight-action crankbaits. The medium sizes will be more productive for numbers of fish.

The Spoonplug is an excellent deep running lure. However, they need help to get down to the depths described here. The Keel sinker helps to get it down without restricting the Spoonplugs action. The 800 Series travel about twenty-five feet deep

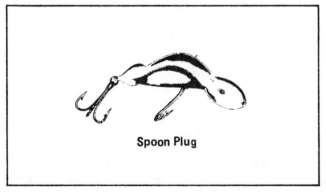

Spoon Plug

without additional help of sinkers. Depth is important. Use extra sinkers to achieve productive depths.

Wire line helps to get that lure deeper, quicker. Try to get small to medium lures down deep for numbers of fish and large lures down for a possible big fish.

F3   LAKES DURING SUMMER; Post-Summer Large Bait Methods

Large bait is six to twelve inches long, anything larger is "monster-bait". You may fish for a few years before catching a walleye on a fifteen inch chub or sucker. If you can handle that, good luck!

There are two times of the year that I use the ten

BIG FISH don't come fast nor easy. Art Moraski caught this walleye while trolling slowly with a jig and large live-bait.

inch or larger size bait: post-summer and late fall. Post-summer because of the numbers of large walleye in deep water, and the late fall because large bait is natural to the environment.

When using large bait for walleyes work very slowly. If trolling, troll slowly. Often times a large walleye will strike at the bait much like a muskie does: from the side. It carries the bait off, stops and then starts to inhale it. You must give the fish time. If using artificials, set the hook immediately.

Some fishermen will use live-bait harnesses . . . that makes the bait look wired for execution. A walleye has to be overly-active to take a bait with all the junk attached to it. The lesser amount of wire and gadgets on the bait, the better the chances of enticing a big fish. The walleye can't think, but neither does it have suicidal tendencies. Ten pound test monofilament will suffice in most situations. Use a number four, six or eight sharp forged steel hook (the actual size will depend on the size of bait used) and sinker that will enable you to work the required depths. Insert the hook through the mouth of the minnow. That's all there is to it.

When using a salamander hook it through the mouth. This will work when drifting, or slowly trolling. Should you want to "still-fish" use the same baits, but hook them through the back — just behind the dorsal fin.

While trolling with artificial lures I don't use wire leaders unless fishing a lake that has an exceptional number of northern pike in it, and I am fishing for monster pike. The biggest down-fall of artificial lure fishermen is not keeping the hooks sharp. Another is purchasing cheap line that may be a year or two old and has started to break down. Finally, lines will start to show wear and tear, especially within the first five feet from the lure. A smart fisherman will snip off four or five feet of line every so often, retie his lure and continue fishing. Which is better, losing a five or six dollar lure, a fish of a lifetime, or snipping off a few feet of line?

The artificial lure market has exploded into an array of fancy coloring and cloned baits. An example is Bagleys (bluegill) bream. It looks so much like a bluegill that I wonder if live bluegills would be able to tell the difference. To the fisherman, it might mean a bit of confusion. Does one have to renovate his tackle box; will the old ones still work; will the new baits revolutionize fishing and which of the new baits is better?

For sight feeders, I believe the new lures will add fish to the stringer. Choose lures that represent the forage that is available in the lakes that you fish. But, in little or no light situations, I haven't seen any improvement over the older types of lures. Vibration is a greater factor. Walleyes relate to sound as well as sight. Sound is a medium of communication in water. The slightest sound travels a long distance in water. While fishing in deep water, the long slim baits seem to be more productive than the short fat ones. Tight-action crankbaits

Bagley Bream

create more sound than the loose-action cranks. In the darkness of depth, visual contact is not made until the lure is within a very short distance of the hunter. I caught a ten pound walleye once while twitching a Rapala (CD-9) in twenty-two feet of water. In that case, visual contact did make a difference.

The migratory walleye remains in deep water until either lack of oxygen forces them to move to shallower levels or the baitfish move to shallow water. The weed-orientated walleye remains in the shallows.

G1   LAKES DURING FALL; Early Fall
              The Hot Spell

To understand what happens and when it happens you must have general knowledge of the lake that is to be fished. It may seem complicated at first but it is very simple. Assuming that all of the lake types described have an abundance of walleye, these are the general rules (realizing that there are exceptions to every rule):

SHALLOW WATER LAKES, MAY BE WEED CHOKED OR BARREN BUT CONNECTED TO A RIVER SYSTEM: During early fall, shallow bays with weeds, or a sand bottom become hot spots for a short period of time before fall turn-over. Turn-over is just a time period in this case because shal-

AN AVERAGE Lake Koshkonong walleye caught on Mister Twister Sassy Shad with spinner.

low water lakes have a turn-over but don't stratify. Shallow rock bars, and riprap areas become dynamite. A perfect example of this type of lake, lies in Jefferson Co., Wisconsin. The lake is Koshkonong. Its maximum depth is approximately eight feet, and it is a walleye factory. Most fish taken are between a pound and three pounds, but there are substantial catches of fish over five pounds and some up to twelve pounds. It is fed by a river system and springs, has dark water, few weeds, but some sand and rock piles. Usually during the month of September, walleyes can be found in the shallow water bays and obstructions found in the lake. From there, the walleyes make their way toward whatever deep water is available and into the river system.

LAKES THAT HAVE A GREATER PERCENTAGE OF SHALLOW WATER, WITH A LOT OF WEEDS: The number of walleyes residing in shallow water is great, althrough the year. During the

early part of fall, the migratory walleyes move into the shallows and feed quite heavily. The actual hot-spell is brief, lasting two weeks at most, unless the weather is fair and stable for a longer period of time. If there is enough deep water, fall turn-over will affect the location of walleyes.

LAKES THAT HAVE A GREATER PERCENTAGE OF MEDIUM DEPTH WATERS, FEW WEEDS AND WITHOUT A SUBSTANTIAL AMOUNT OF SUSPENDED FORAGE: There is a migration of walleyes into the shallows for a brief period during early fall. Gravel, rock, sand and weeds are the best areas for fishing. If the water is clear, the dropoffs are best; if dark, the shallow water flats of the contents described should be fished.

LAKES THAT HAVE A GREAT PERCENTAGE OF DEEP WATER, A LOT OF SUSPENDED FORAGE (CISCO, TULLIBEE, ALEWIFE, SHAD, ETC.), AND MIGHT CONTAIN TROUT: There appears to be little movement into the shallows during early fall. Areas where shallow water walleyes reside may be productive. The migratory walleye tends to remain in deep water, with some night movements. The hot-spots for fishing (for the migratory fish) are areas where the level (depth level) of baitfish and vertical structures meet *(Illustration 207, Fig. 1)*. In the same lake there might be a resident school of shallow water fish *(Fig. 2)*. Explore the shallows where bottom conditions offer food and cover. If the water is clear fish deeper; if dark fish shallow. Weed bars become both day and night hot-spots during late August and early September in the northern part of the country. Yearling perch are grown to adequate size and attract some walleyes to the shallows.

The hot-spell lasts for a relatively short period of time and can be turned off completely by unstable weather conditions. Cold fronts have a very negative effect on the walleye that inhabits the shallows. The hot-spell ends with the progression of fall turnover.

G2   LAKES DURING FALL; Early Fall
           Understanding Fall Turnover

Nature has a unique way of supplying her lakes with oxygen. There are two turnover periods; fall

ILLUSTRATION 207

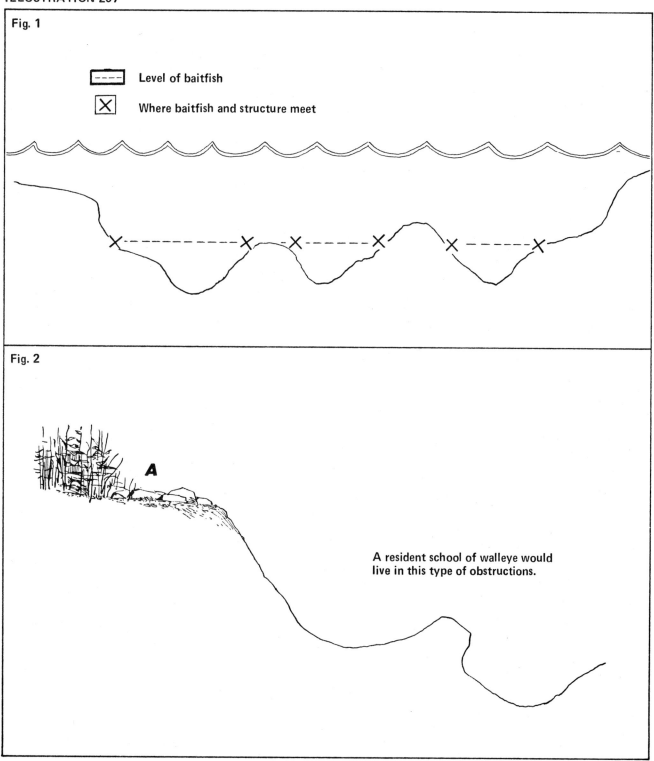

Fig. 1

☐╌╌╌ Level of baitfish

☒ Where baitfish and structure meet

Fig. 2

A

A resident school of walleye would live in this type of obstructions.

turnover and spring turnover. During the summer, many lakes stratify in layers of temperature change. The greatest temperature change occurs at a level called the "thermocline". Waters above the thermocline are usually oxygen filled warmer waters; below it, lesser amounts of oxygen are present (that amount is dependent upon the amount of rotting, oxygen-stealing vegetation that is found in the lake). During fall, air temperatures and surface water temperatures start to drop. The cooler top water sinks to its own density level, breaking up the stratification of water. At the same time, wind helps to mix the lake up. This creates a fresh re-oxygenated environment. It takes a number of cool days and nights to get the process going in full swing. Medium depth lakes may experience false turnover many times before the lasting affect is present. The shallow lakes experience some turnover but the fish activity is slowed down due to changes and unstable weather.

Often times a fisherman suspects fall turnover is taking place, but does not know what to look for to confirm it. These are some of the tell-tale signs: the shallows have very little baitfish activity, at times, none are to be found; frequently the lake looks like it's steaming at night (cooling off); on a calm day, the water appears to be moving; dead vegetation shows up at the surface; the lake may reek with odor; fishing is tough; and there is only a slight temperature change between the surface and about thirty feet of water. If all of these signs are present and it is during the late summer or early fall, fall turnover is taking place.

Spring turnover takes place at the breaking up of ice. The ice cold top water sinks and the wind helps to homogenize the lake. Fishing during these times is truly tough. The turnover periods represent a great change in the walleyes environment.

G3   LAKES DURING FALL; Early Fall
Scattering of the troops

The fall turnover period lasts only a few days, but the affect of fall turnover may last two or more weeks. We can conclude some facts by the location of baitfish and actual fish catches. The facts are: most baitfish tend to go very deep or sus-

pend; there is some shallow water movement during warm fall days; walleyes that are caught seem to be scattered, caught at different depth levels (some are caught while suspended) and hardly schooled; most of the larger walleyes are caught in deep water; the shallow water weed walleyes have moved out, with few remaining, even at night; some walleyes caught will have aquatic insects in them, suggesting that they are feeding on deep water mud flats; when associated with vertical structure, steep dropoffs are better than gradual inclines.

During this time of the year I have caught walleyes deeper than any other time period. An occasional perch has found its way to my live box, caught in fifty feet of water and beyond. The deepest that I have caught a walleye was eighty feet of water, on a trout lake. Over the years there has been very little information available concerning the location or fish catching methods relating to turnover walleyes, however, information in the Lake Erie Section will surprise you.

Minnows and large bait seem to work best. Slow methods of presentation are essential. Work the deep waters at the base of vertical structures and mud flats that are near to known summer hotspots.

G4   LAKES DURING FALL; Early Fall
Lake Jumping

Shallow bodies of water react to changes in temperatures much quicker than large bodies of water. A week of hot weather during fall has a great effect on shallow lakes. They could turn out to be hot-spots for a short period of time, while large bodies of water may be turned off. The opposite is also true. While a shallow lake is turned off because of sudden changes in water temperatures, a large lake (depth wise) takes longer to react . . . walleye fishing may be exceptionally good on that lake.

Just before turnover, fish the shallow lakes following the shallow water movements of the hotspell. As turnover progresses and cold water effects the shallower lakes go to the deeper lakes and fish them until the action slows down. Go back to the shallow lakes after turnover to try and pick up on the late fall movements, then fish the deep lakes to catch the walleyes that are following their forage (fall spawning forage) into the shallows. With some practice and the availability of different types of lakes, a fisherman can stay on the peak of activity on various lakes throughout fall. It may not be a bonanza, but you will stay on fish.

If you are totally confused and have no idea as to what stage a lake may be in, try the following — spend a half a day on a medium to shallow body of water, then switch to a deep body of water for the remainder of the day. Pick prime structure and work from the shallows out to deep water. Note the depth where fish contact has been made and pursue your fishing accordingly. As fishing comes to a halt on that type of lake, go to the extreme opposite. Often times a fisherman can get his information from a good bait shop. Find out two things: what kind of lake the fish are coming from and the depth of water that they are being caught in. The structures and tools you already have from this text. The other alternative is to fish a river system *(covered in Section III).*

H1 LAKES DURING FALL; Fall
The Slow Come-back

Bone-chilling days and frost-covered nights are reminders that summer is gone and fall is here. With proper clothing it is a very comfortable time of year to be fishing (when the weather cooperates). With water temperatures between the high and low forties, walleyes start their slow progression into the shallow water again. Their movement is slightly different than those of summer movements. The fall movements are associated with steep dropoffs *(illustration 208, Fig. 1)*, shorter feeding sprees and a reluctance to stay in shallow water. The better structures are ones that have a fast dropoff, preferably rock, gravel or weeds and have a sand or hard bottom base, providing a flat. Dropoffs associated with weeds become excellent areas *(Fig. 2)*. Steep points of rock and gravel that extend out from a point of land are good structures to fish.

Small walleyes are schooled again and the big females are grouping. A few active fish can be taken from the same spot. Usually lakes clear up by this time and other cover is needed to hold fish. That

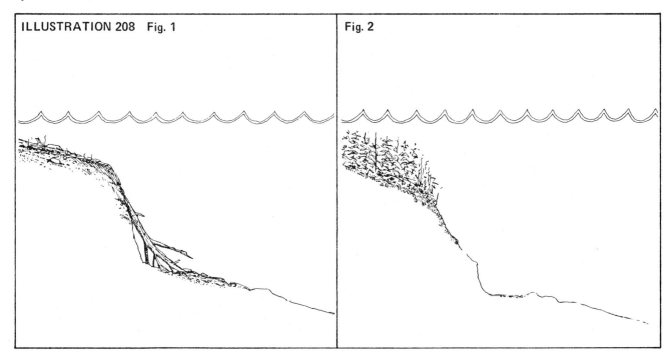

ILLUSTRATION 208   Fig. 1

Fig. 2

cover may be the darkness of a steep dropoff or security of big boulders or rocks. Weeds that bait-fish are found in will hold some walleye. Deep water weedbeds are excellent. Deep water in this instance means fifteen and eighteen feet of water.

On some lakes sand flats that are near shore and bordered by a fast dropoff on the lake side become very excellent fishing areas. These sand flats range from five to fifteen feet in depth. The clearer the water, the less chance of it being a hot-spot. On dark water lakes, give them a try.

The period of time between fall turnover and full swing of the come-back may take as long as a month. That greatly depends on the weather. If the weather turns cold gradually it may take three weeks. If there is a sudden cold weather stretch that lasts for a couple of weeks, it may take two weeks. If the weather turns hot and cold every other day, it may take a month or more. The determining weather factor is stability, whether it be warm or cold. The trick is to follow peak-activity through the lakes and regions.

TO FOLLOW the peak activity can produce fish like these caught by Spence Petros and Ron Warzyinski.

H2   LAKES DURING FALL; Fall
Following Peak Activity

Following peak activity by lake and region is a very important key to successful walleye fishing. Now that you understand the difference between the shallow lakes and deep lakes it is also important to make an adjustment for locality or region. To give an example of this, let's divide Minnesota, Wisconsin or Michigan into thirds (*Illustration 209*). The lower portion of these states is "Region I", the mid-section is "Region II" and the upper portion is "Region III", going from south to north. The distance may be averaged at about six hundred miles, giving each region approximately two hundred miles. There may be twenty degree or more air temperature differences between the southern most portion and the northern portion. This will have an affect on the water temperatures. Obviously the southern lakes will warm quicker than the northern lakes. We could choose any part of the activity cycle that a lake goes through to show what happens and how to follow peak activity, but for this example we will choose "spawning" to show the south to north progression, and "fall turnover" to show the north to south progression.

Weather must be taken into consideration. For this example, the weather during spring is a slow warming trend and during fall, a slow cooling trend. In the illustration, we are comparing two types of lakes in each "region", a small shallow lake, and a large deep lake. The time periods are approximate and change with weather and water temperatures:

SPAWNING ACTIVITY: In "Region I" the small shallow lake number (1) should experience spawning activity at the end of April; next, in "Region II" spawning takes place on number (2) at late April or early May; then "Region I" Lake (3) starts spawning activity (it's deeper and takes longer for the water temperatures to rise): then, in "Region III" lake number (4) starts approximately mid-May; in "Region II" lake number (5) starts about mid-May; the last one is "Region III" lake number (6), where the spawning activity might not start until late-May. As you can see, spawning occurs much sooner in lakes of the south-

ILLUSTRATION 209

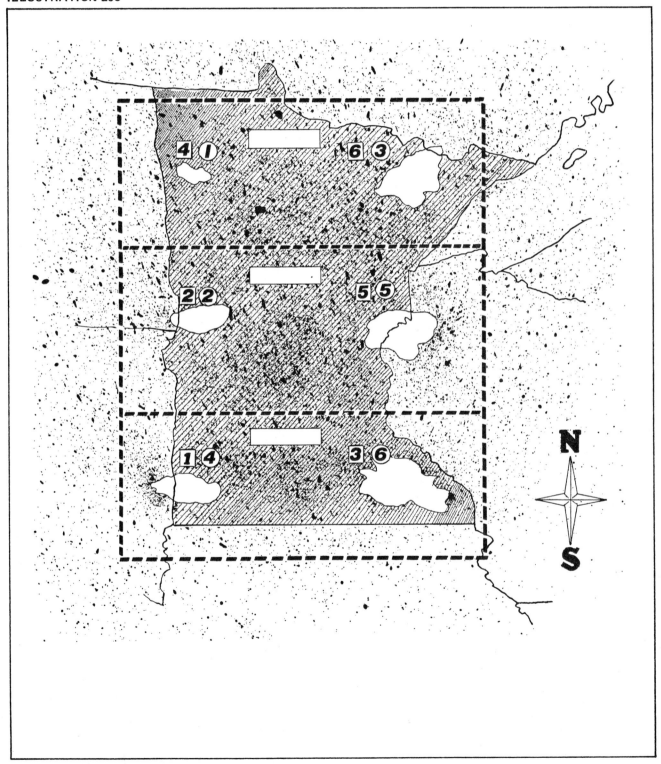

ern portions of the state, and closer to summer in the northern portions. If the weather were to be very hot during May, the entire cycle could transpire within two weeks, or it could take a lot longer during a cold May. You could follow the active fishing days of summer by the same method — as long as you know the approximate weather conditions.

EARLY FALL TURNOVER: During fall, work backwards. If a cooling trend started from the north and worked its way south, then the following holds true. Fall turnover will take place in "Region III" lake number (1) first, because it is shallow and will react to the cool temperature changes first. It may happen during late August; next in "Region II" lake number (2) during late August or early September; then, "Region III" lake number (3) during early September; then "Region I" lake number (4) during mid-September; then, "Region II" lake number (5) during mid-September and finally; "Region I" lake number (6) during late September. The activity periods might not follow an exact pattern but you can get pretty close by plotting it out and checking with bait shops in the different areas.

This is extremely helpful when planning a vacation. For instance, if planning a vacation during late May, it may be wise to vacation in the southern portion of the state where the walleyes might be setting up in its summer patterns; and at the tail end of June, if vacationing in the extreme northern portion of either of these states. Plus, check out the shallow lakes versus large deep lakes depending on the time of year and activity cycle.

The information that you have just read is one of the secrets of many successful walleye anglers. Don't beat your brains out on dead water, follow the patterns by switching lakes or fishing areas. It's much easier than becoming frustrated by not catching fish!

H3   LAKES DURING FALL; Fall
              Cold Water Fishing

One cannot tell what the weather's going to be like. A likely assumption is that it is going to be cold, possibly windy with an occasional sprinkle.

It is extremely uncomfortable when you are not prepared for the worst. Most of the anglers that I know say, "If you can keep your ears, hands and feet warm and dry, the rest of your body will follow suit". With due respect, I have to add, that having your body sweat inside from too many clothes is just as bad. Here is a short check list to help overcome the cold days of fall:

Snowmobile suit
Thermo underwear and rain suit
Several pair of cheap gloves
Thermos bottle of hot soup or coffee
Insulated boots
Ear muffs or knit cap that covers the ears
Face mask for running the lake
Warm socks (thick) possible bread wrapper
  on your feet
Zip-on life-jacket
Minnow dip-net
Hand warmer
Parka
A towel
A carpet for the bottom of an aluminum boat
A seat cushion for aluminum or wooden seats
A moisture cream for wind burn face
Chap stick for cracked lips
A turtle neck shirt or sweater helps to
  keep your body warm
Wear clothes that fit you

Many of these items can become a part of your cold weather gear. I keep my cold weather gear in a separate duffle bag and keep it in my automobile — just in case. Personally, I prefer the two piece snowmobile suit so I can take one piece off, should the weather change. Many of my friends like the one-piece, it is a matter of personal preference. I am right-handed, so I cut the finger-tips off of my right-hand glove, giving me the ability to feel messages transmitted through the line. Carrying extra pairs of gloves comes in handy should the pair you are using become wet. Don't over-expose yourself, stop for a shore lunch and warm up. Besides, it gives you a chance to review your game plan.

The cold water period and its good fishing lasts until ice-up. Movement of schooling fish is quite noticeable. The walleyes move along, stop at hold-

ILLUSTRATION 210

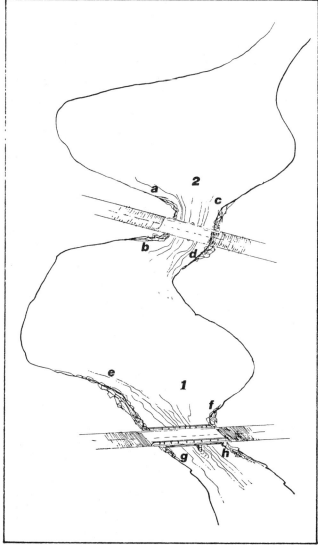

the possibility of current. Looking at *Illustration 210,* area (I) is more likely to have movement of water than area (II), so area (I) would be the best area to work first. Work each area denoted by (A), (B), (C), (D), and the stretch of (E), (F), (G) and (H). If these bridges are roadways they are likely to have a lot of rocks at the base, good structure for walleyes to relate to.

The wind-swept shores will have a build up of plankton and other aquatic insects that are at the mercy of the wind. Baitfish tend to follow these movements because it is their food source. The resident walleye population of that area will also follow their food. The rock and timber shorelines are usually attractive areas for walleyes. You can fish the area from a boat or from the shore effectively, with a jig and minnow combination, live bait or artificial minnow imitation lures. Walleye movement is greater during early morning, late afternoon and evening, and at night.

I1   LAKES DURING FALL; Late Fall
Fishing Large Lakes

Late fall is the time to fish the large, deep lakes. The typical large deep lake may have any number of these characteristics: a great percentage by volume of deep water; a substantial suspended forage population; a lot of rock, sand, boulders and few weeds; usually clear water; may sustain a good trout or smallmouth bass population; have a number of underground springs in the lake; not be known as a particularly good walleye lake, but fishermen will talk about the big walleyes that they have seen during spawning; may contain depths of eighty feet or more.

These lakes have a greater chance of producing large walleye during late fall than any other type. The weather is usually cold and rather unpleasant to fish in, but the rewards can be profound.

Don't let the size of the lake scare you. Treat each section of a large lake as if it were a number of small deep water lakes. The suspended forage populations will build up on the side of the lake that gets a predominant wind. However, it is important to realize that the suspended forage represents an astronomical number of fish. There-

ing spots, feed then move on. The well structured areas may receive fish movement regularly. The fisherman interprets this as hot and cold spots. He will catch several fish over a short period of time, then the spot goes dead. The fish may have migrated, and the fisherman doesn't catch fish until another school moves in (although the possibility of the fish turning off for a period is also likely). This is particularly true of areas where current is involved. Bottleneck areas of lakes usually have some current. Bridges and narrow lake areas are the cause. The tighter the bottleneck the greater

ILLUSTRATION 211

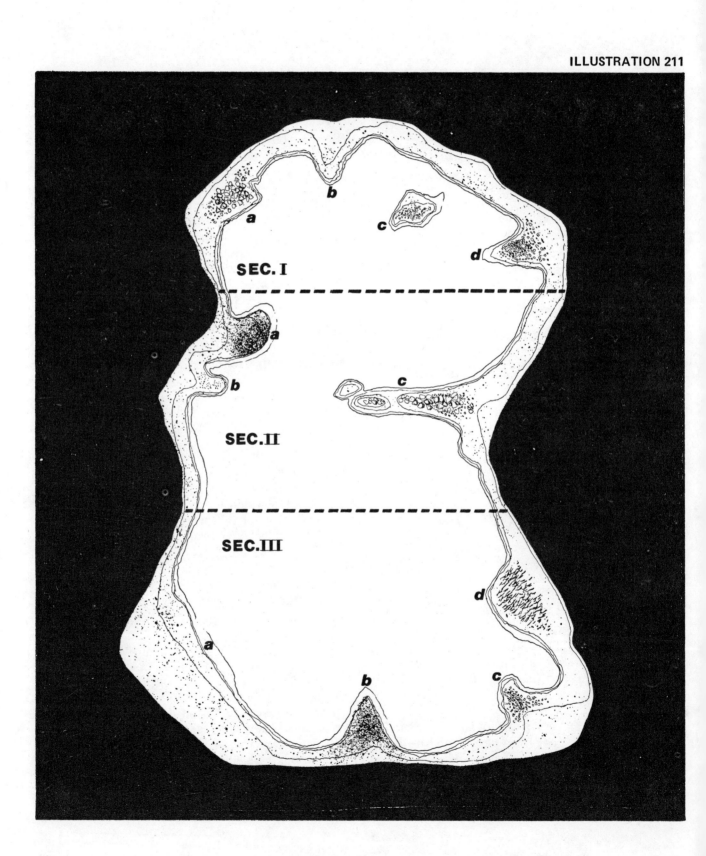

by each section of the lake will have a substantial number of fish present, with a greater number relating to the wind receiving side of structure in each portion of the lake, by virtue of a horizontal plane. Suspended forage such as cisco moves on a basic horizontal plane. That level moves vertically according to changes in water temperatures and food supply. Most of the forage fish species are prisoners of temperate zones. Occasionally a fisherman will catch a cisco, bring it to the surface rapidly and have the fish die almost immediately. In most cases, the level of suspended forage of a particular species will hold a horizontal plane throughout the lake showing little or no variation in depth unless there are tremendous deep water temperature changes from one side of the lake to the other. The forage fish don't stack up on structure vertically like crappies do. It is a common occurence to have eight foot thick horizontal band of forage fish stretched out over a ¼ mile.

As water temperatures drop, these fall spawners rise to shallower (in surface depth) water. They relate to prime spawning areas per area of the lake in which they are present. Each of the prime spawning areas will receive their portion of fall spawners by specie preference. Cisco may spawn in one area and whitefish in another. In dividing up the lake *(Illustration 211)*, section it off into thirds or more. In "Section I" (A), (B), (C) and (D) could have all of the proper elements to attract fall spawners, but it is possible that the forage might only use one of these areas. Sand, rock and gravel attracts fall spawners. Maybe one of them will be suitable enough to attract fish. In "Section II" (A) is not the prime area but (B) and (C) have potential. In "Section III" (A) and (C) show greater potential than (B) or (D). Dividing up the lake in this manner, gives you a sound method of approach. The effect of the suspended forage on walleyes is astonishing. Realizing where the suspended forage is during late fall is extremely important to the success of fishing these types of lakes.

I2   LAKES DURING FALL; Late Fall
Effects Of Suspended Forage

Fall affords the best opportunity to catch large

walleyes. In the deep lake mentioned, the greatest percentage of walleye relate to the suspended forage, often times living in a suspended state (suspended walleyes are discussed in the Lake Erie section). For the walleye it is the easiest game in town. The law of survival reads, "follow your food". In essence it means, when the forage fish spawn in shallow water, those hog walleyes are nearby. At night I have witnessed large numbers of big walleyes moving about schools of spawning suspended forage in the shallows on sand and gravel bars. Occasionally the cisco will dimple the surface waters during the evening at spawning time. Surface water temperatures are usually in the early forties.

During the day, fish those structures that are near to the forage spawning areas. Those hog walleyes will hold tightly to the deep dropoffs associated with the spawning areas. At night the spawning grounds come alive with fish. The spawning forage doesn't always relate to super shallow water for spawning. In some instances they may spawn in depths of fifteen feet or more, but are almost always on sand, gravel and rock flats.

After spawning, the majority of the suspended forage move off to deeper waters. A great portion of the young stay in shallow water for some time to come. In affect this moves a great number of walleyes deep again, while a number of them stay shallow, feeding the new hatch. The feeding spree could last till a good formation of ice has formed, thus one of the reasons for good walleye fishing at first ice.

Use larger than normal live bait during late fall. There is a good chance of catching large fish and the large bait attracts a lot of attention. When trolling, use large artificial lures and troll slowly. Minnow imitation lures are excellent for trolling or casting. Walleyes will be shallowest at night.

I3   LAKES DURING FALL; Late Fall
Re-grouping

A large number of big walleye follow their food source out to deeper waters. They wolf-pack the forage in small groups as a method of feeding. Smaller class walleyes and some large ones remain

SCHOOLING FISH are usually close to the same size and age group.

in shallow waters feeding on the new hatch. Near ice-up perch (and crappies) start to move into the shallows to garbage up on the new arrivals. This creates another food base for the remaining walleyes. Yearling perch are still in areas where vegetation exists. Some areas of the shallows provide an excellent food source for walleyes and other predators. The dramatic split may occur at this time on this type of lake. The weed walleye takes up resistence in shallow water due to the renewed food base; the migratory walleye moves in at night, feeds and moves out during the daylight hours because of the lack of cover in the clear water and; the deep water walleye follows its food supply (the suspended forage) back out to deeper waters.

On the deep water lakes described, the percentage of walleye population may break down somewhat like this:

70% deep water walleye

10% weed walleye

20% migratory walleye

The lake that has a lot of weeds, little or no suspended forage, but does have a high percentage of deep water, may break down as follows:

10% deep water walleye

60% weed walleye

30% migratory walleye

Grouping would not be as evident on this type of lake. The food source will determine where the walleyes will be. Understand it, follow it, and the location of walleyes will become much clearer.

The walleye has to live on the suitable food in its environment. The actual presentation methods and various lures on the market won't help you to catch fish unless fish are present!

I4   LAKES DURING FALL; Late Fall
S-L-O-W Methods For Big Fish

Fishing slow is a difficult task for most active fishermen. It is especially true during the cold water periods. Slow fishing veterans find themselves glued to a spot, most of the time being painfully nonproductive. A game plan must be established if you hope to produce on a consistent basis.

Plan before-hand. Figure out which areas are most likely to produce fish. In this case, the steep dropoffs in conjunction with good inshore structure are important. Pick out the areas that show the greatest amount of promise: points; the narrows of a lake; bottle neck situations; saddles; all in relationship to known fall spawners prime areas, or known walleye hot-spots. Calculate the amount of time that you will spend on each spot. If you wrote it down on paper it should read something like this:

Spot A: Still-fish around the point with red-tail chubs for one hour. Check out fifteen, twenty, twenty-five and thirty-five foot depth levels. Slowly troll around point and along the immediate dropoff for half an hour. Move to spot B.

Spot B: Slowly troll along the sand flat edge, covering the fifteen to twenty-five foot depths. Still-fish where fish contact has been made. No contact, move to spot C.

Spot C: Slowly troll at the base of the rock slide where sand meets the rocks. Work the twenty-five to fifty foot depths. Spend no more than an hour. Still-fish if there is the slightest pick-up. Move to spot D.

Spot D: Fan cast with live bait and work slowly around the point. Map indicates a saddle. Work the base in between the points. Move to the outside point and slow troll with live bait. Spend no more than an hour. If there hasn't been any action, move to the extreme opposite lake-type and set up a new plan.

This game plan was set up because your first choice of lakes was a very clear water lake, thus, starting at the fifteen foot level. It would have taken from five to six hours to cover it fairly well. A smaller lake of the extreme opposite (and nearby) could take a lot less time, giving you a full day of fishing and a chance to find active fish. The full execution of a game plan helps to make the day interesting and productive. It also cures the boredom of slow fishing. With map and game plan in hand, the fisherman has a reason for everything that he does on the water.

The live bait that is used for fishing for big walleyes is usually six to twelve inches long. Some of the better minnows are: large chubs, suckers, golden shiners, river shiners, large mud minnows (better in flowages), and dead smelt. Don't throw your dead bait away. Hook it on a jig and work them just as you would work a smaller jig and minnow. If the bait reeks from odor or gets torn up from northern pike, discard it. Walleyes are highly sensitive to the smell of northern pike. Should a northern pike strike at your bait, change baits.

When the sucker or chub dies, take the sinker off of your line. Stick some sinkers into the baits mouth. Force it down with a pen or pencil, it adds weight to the bait and takes some of the distraction away from your line. Hook a single number four or six hook through the minnows mouth. Now you're all set to go. Cast the bait towards the dropoff and work it back to the boat. Let the bait settle, then snap your wrist. The bait zig-zags upwards and descends back down. This action simulates a dying minnow.

With the innovation of reels that are capable of high speed retrieves, it makes it difficult to retrieve slowly. If you have an old reel that has a three to one retrieve, use it during the times that require slow fishing. As time goes on, retrieving becomes a sub-conscious act. A reel with a lower gear ratio helps to slow down the retrieve.

Fishing slow is an art that must be developed by the fisherman. The walleye has a chance to examine the bait before attacking. The walleye might notice a thick diameter line; the smell of a human; the extra junk (harness) wrapped around the minnow; the flashy swivels on the line; the outrageous size of a hook; or bulky sinkers on the line. All of these items must be taken into consideration. An actively feeding fish will strike out of blind, ferocious hunger; although not self-sacrificing. When in a neutral to negative disposition, the fisherman has to entice the walleye to strike, and take all of the necessary precautions.

It is seldom that you will run across an entire school of active fish. Generally, a number of fish in the school will become active. They will feed causing a chain reaction with more fish in the school. As the sense of danger arises, the reluctant fish discontinue feeding. They are the tough fish to catch. Most of the time, the fisherman seeks another spot. It is a wise decision. However, when in a big fish school, it pays to refine your methods and stick around a while. The presentation of the bait is important. Get the excess junk off of the line and fish slowly.

I5   LAKES DURING FALL; Late Fall
The Bait

The bait is the point of attack, the most important link between you and the fish. It should look good, smell good, and be presented correctly. Often times the fisherman doesn't realize the negative factors that he adds to his bait. Here's a little story that points out negative factors.

"Curt Goes Fishing"

Curt decides to go fishing on Lake Kitty, because it is known for its huge late fall walleyes. On the way Curt stops for some large chubs. He grabs his large white bucket, the one that Uncle Louie, the glue factory worker (Neg. 1), gave him. Curt purchases four dozen large chubs (Neg. 2) and tells the salesman to put them into his five gallon pail.

Happily on his way, Curt suddenly realizes he's almost out of gas. So, he stops at a self service station and fills up the jeep and tank in the boat, adds some oil and pays the man. (Neg. 3)

Finally he reaches Lake Kitty. It's a beautiful day. It's hot for a late fall day. The bugs are pesty so Curt sprays on some bug spray (Neg. 4). Now he's ready to fish. Curt motors out to his prospective big fish area. Checks out the point and decides

to fish it. Curt wants the biggest minnow he can find, so hand-in-bucket (Neg. 5) he chases the minnows around endlessly, grabbing one then another until he is convinced that he's found the largest one (Neg. 6). While trying to hook the slippery devil it pops out of his hand and squirms on the floor of the boat (Neg. 7). It's like chasing a bar of soap around the bathtub. Finally Curt has a good hold on the minnow and inserts the hook.

Curt is going to slowly back-troll around the point. He lowers the minnow into the water, (Neg. 8) right next to the boat. Visions of wall-hanging size walleyes start to form in his minds-eye. He is quickly aroused by a sudden jerk, his reaction is to set the hook immediately. The line goes slack and Curt retrieves it, bringing the minnow up next to the motor (Neg. 9). Upon examination, Curt notices a set of teeth marks; one by the head and the other near the tail. More excited than ever he lowers the minnow back down (Neg. 10) right by the motor (Neg. 11), and continues to fish.

Curts fishing day was very unsuccessful. He caught a few northern pike, but no walleye — not even a hit. A very typical story.

The walleye lives in an environment that is filled with sounds, smells and has limited visibility. The sounds are from movement of baitfish; crawling creatures; distress; man's presence; the elements; predator and prey. The smells are of: food, human odors; fish odors; and odors of different creatures that live in the medium of water. They are highly developed senses needed for survival. Thus the negative factors of Curts fishing trip are really important. Here's a review of those negatives.

Neg. 1.   The large white bucket may have some chemical residue in it. Give it a sterile bath, or put a plastic liner in it.

Neg. 2.   Over-crowding the minnows just kills them. A dozen or a dozen and a half would have been enough. Remember, Curt was using large bait.

Neg. 3.   The chance of Curt getting some gas and oil on his hands is 100%. Either go to a full-service station and let the attendant do the work (even though your change will have the attendants gas residue on) or wash your hands with a good detergent thoroughly.

Neg. 4. After using a bug spray or lotion, wash your hands with a strong detergent if you plan to handle live bait.

Neg. 5. The lesser the possibility of human scent or chemical scent on the minnows the better. Use a dip-net and moisten your hands. It is harder to control the minnow with damp hands, but the transference of smell is minimal.

Neg. 6. Use a dip-net whenever possible.

Neg. 7. Almost all gas powered boats will at some time or another have some gas and oil residue on the bottom. A minnow that is dropped squirms around and picks up the odors. The safest place to hook the minnow is near the front of the boat or over the bucket.

Neg. 8. Few fishermen give thought to this one. They take all of the precautions necessary, then lower the minnow into the water going through a gas slick. On a calm day you can notice the rainbow of colors that surrounds the motor and immediate boat area. Instead of lowering the minnow right through the gas slick, cast it out six or seven feet and let it swing back toward the boat while in the water.

Neg. 9. Again Curt brought the minnow up through the gas slick. Put the motor in neutral (he was back-trolling) and bring the minnow up at the side of the boat, at a full rods length.

Neg. 10. Chances are that a northern pike has attacked Curts minnow. Northerns leave a very distinct smell (you can even smell it). Discard the minnow and start with a fresh one ... or fish for northerns.

Neg. 11. Curt lowered the minnow through the gas slick again. It has an undesirable taste, and leaves an undesirable smell in the water.

An active school of ferocious feeding fish may not care about any of the negative factors. In a very competitive atmosphere there's little time to care, but when slow fishing to a neutral or negative minded fish, the plusses have to be on your side in order for you to be successful on a consistent basis.

J1   LAKES DURING WINTER; Early Ice
Safety Precautions

Fishing during early and late ice is usually good but also dangerous. New ice is safer than old ice. Old ice gets air bubbles as deterioration sets in. This creates a dangerous situation. It is generally accepted that an inch of new ice is not safe; two to three inches of ice supports an ice fisherman; four inches of ice is fairly safe; and five or more inches of ice will support a snowmobile. No matter how thick, be careful when pursuing ice fishing as a hobby. Watch for gray or black ice, usually indicating a soft spot. There may be springs in the lake and the ice is usually thinner above them. Occasionally, ice shifts due to weight and pressures. The result is an upheaval or actual split in the ice. These spots can be hazardous, so be careful.

There are a few items that will help in case of an emergency. Take a bucket (for sitting on) and fill it with these items: a small amount of sand to spread out for secure footing; at least fifty feet of rope; a plastic bag filled with a few pairs of dry gloves. And take along a seat cushion. These items may save your life one day.

Ice fishing can be a lot of fun for those who dare to meddle in nature's ice-box. Common sense must prevail in every situation. Over exertion can lead to heart attacks. Over dressing can lead to discomfort and illness. The body sweats and can get chilled easily. So enjoy ... but be careful.

J2   LAKES DURING WINTER; Early Ice
The Equipment

The total investment that ice fishermen spend on

their equipment hardly scratches the surface compared to an open water fishermans investment. For most ice fishermen, a few jigging rods, some bait, a sled and bucket will suffice. The open water fisherman has capital investment tied up in boat, motor, and trailer, not to mention the hundreds of dollars of fishing tackle. Let's review the essential equipment used for ice fishing for walleye:

Fig. (1) The "Ice Chisel" or "Spud" is a heavy bar that has a blunt almost sharp edge. It is used during the thin ice periods. A fisherman can make a hole quite easily when the ice is less than four inches thick. You must hang on to the rope while chopping or you might lose it when breaking through the ice.

Fig. (2) A "Ice Skimmer" is used for clearing the ice from the hole drilled in the ice. It also comes in handy for breaking the thin layer of ice that forms in the hole.

Fig. (3) There are different types of ice augers. The one shown is the most common. They are available in various lengths and blade sizes. Most walleye fishermen will use the six or eight inch size (the diameter of the blade). With sharp blades you can drill through six inches of ice within a minute or two. Other types of augers include the gas driven auger, and an auger that has a shovel for a blade.

Fig. (4) Many fishermen lose their catch while trying to bring it through the hole. The gaff when properly used and sharpened provides a means of

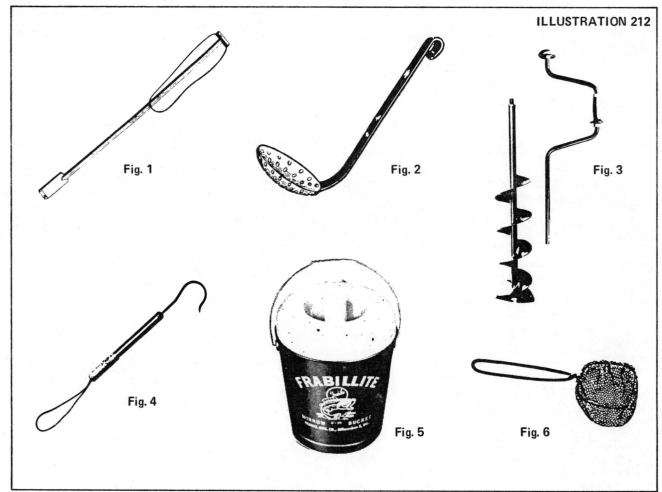

ILLUSTRATION 212

Fig. 1

Fig. 2

Fig. 3

Fig. 4

FRABILLITE

Fig. 5

Fig. 6

pulling the fish through the hole with little effort. Bring the walleyes head to the hole opening. In one quick motion, slip the gaff behind its gill cover or through the chin and pull. Don't stop pulling until the fish is all the way through the hole.

Fig. (5) The minnow bucket is a must for the live bait fisherman. I want to point out that there is greater savings in purchasing a good one to start with. The inexpensive foam buckets break too easily, especially in the cold weather. Replacement costs, over a period of time, would have allowed you to purchase a good one in the first place.

Fig. (6) The dip net is hardly noticed, until you forget to bring it. Then ice cold fingers remind you of its importance. The dip net is not only useful for removing minnows from the bucket, but

can also be used to skim the hole.

Fig. (7) *Illustration 213*, There are several types of tip-ups available. The one shown has a tripod base and the reel remains under water. It is a nice feature because the reel stays ice free. Another type has the reel above the ice. It is nice on relatively warm winter days because there is less resistance on the spool. Nevertheless, when the reels freeze, the only solution is to get them thawed and dried.

Fig. (8) The ice fishing rod is much different than the fishing rods used during summer fishing. It is short because it isn't used for casting, but it does have enough length to impart action to a jig. The price will vary considerably depending on choice of reels. The reels are quite simple, having

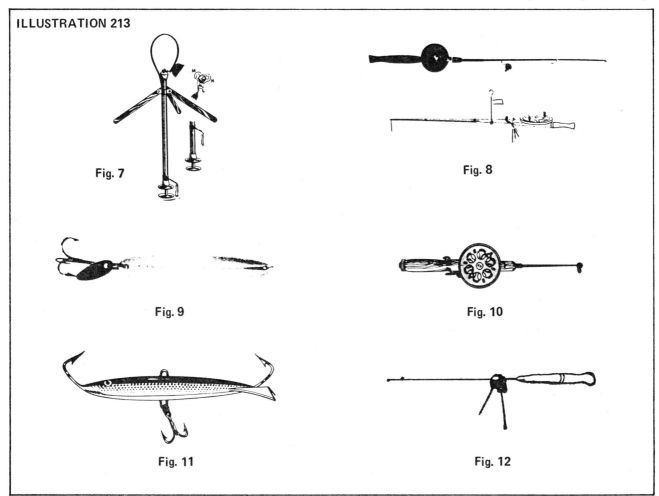

ILLUSTRATION 213

Fig. 7

Fig. 8

Fig. 9

Fig. 10

Fig. 11

Fig. 12

ILLUSTRATION 214

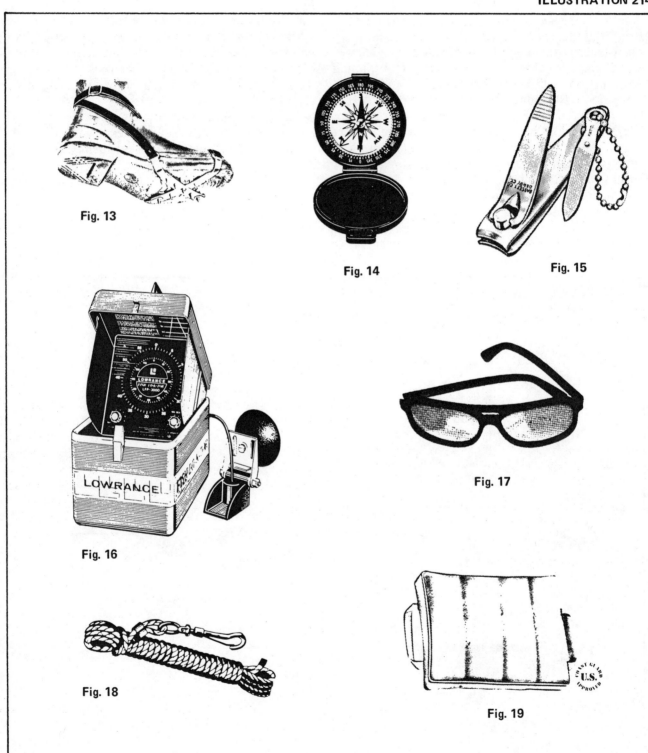

Fig. 13

Fig. 14

Fig. 15

Fig. 16

Fig. 17

Fig. 18

Fig. 19

the drag set by a thumb screw. Walleye fishermen prefer a rod that is a little stiff. This helps when working jigs and larger live bait.

Fig. (9) The Swedish Pimple is one of the most popular walleye fishing baits. It is a slender spoon available in many weights. It's lowered to the bottom, a quick flick of the wrist shoots it upward. With line taut, the Swedish Pimple is lowered back to the bottom. The walleye usually strikes as the bait is falling. Occasionally, a nightcrawler or piece of minnow is attached to the treble hook.

Fig. (10) The Normark Thrumming Rod is unique because there is a thumb button that when pressed moves the rod shaft creating a jigging effect on the lure or bait. It takes little effort to cause the bait to twitch.

Fig. (11) Rapala's "Ice Fishing Jig" is an imitation minnow type bait that is outstanding for walleye fishing. By jigging it up and down, the fisherman can cause the lure to go in circles. Once mastered, the lure will certainly help to fill the stringer with walleyes. It is available in a number of sizes.

Fig. (12) The rubber rod stand is secured to the rod by pressing the wire legs inwards. Then put the rod between the rubber opening, and release the wire legs. It is like a spring loaded clothes pin. The rubber rod stand helps to keep the rod off of the ice and does not interfere with the line when a fish is hooked. They are very inexpensive and allows the fisherman freedom to check on other rods or tip-ups.

Fig. (13) "Creepers" really help to secure footing especially when the ice is relatively free of snow. Keep a pair in your ice sled box. They can be strapped on to any boot or shoe.

Fig. (14) A compass will come in handy when fishing a large lake, or during a snow blizzard. A small inexpensive one is easy to carry.

Fig. (15) A lot of fishermen bite their monofilament line when changing lures. Ask your dentist about it. It really ruins teeth. A nail clipper should appear in every fishermans pocket and tackle box.

Fig. (16) A portable depth finder can be your eyes to the under water world. Use it to find drop-offs, different types of structure and suspended forage fish. To get it to read through the ice, pour a small amount of water or antifreeze on the ice, then hold the transducer tightly against the ice. If the unit does not give a reading, there may be air bubbles present, so slide the transducer back and forth gently. The depth finder works better during early ice and mid-winter, after that there may be many air bubbles and pockets in the ice, so you must find good ice.

Fig. (17) The glare from snow and ice on a sunny day is just about enough to give you a headache and sore eyes. A pair of sunglasses is essential.

Fig. (18) Keep a loosely wound rope in your ice sled box or bucket. Should a fisherman go through the ice, stand approximately twenty feet or more away and toss him one end of the rope. Tell the victim to roll and sprawl out on the ice. Keep pulling him until he is a safe distance from the point of entry.

Fig. (19) A "Coast Guard Approved Cushion" will help in case of an emergency. It is also comfortable to sit on and primarily used to kneel on when skimming the hole or pulling a fish through.

All of the tools are simple to use and help to make fish catching a pleasure. Regular jigs and rigs are also used. Occasionally a fisherman builds his own ice fishing rods from tip sections that may have broken off his summer fishing rods. These fishermen also use regular spinning reels. They are nice to use but just an added expense if purchased solely for ice fishing.

The lures and live bait rigs used are most effective when used at the correct depths. A fisherman may bore several holes before locating fish. Different depths of fishing should be explored prior to relocating to another hole. Depth and speed of descent is extremely important.

The walleye fisherman usually uses four to twelve pound test line. The average line is eight pound test. A lighter line is needed when fishing is tough, and a heavier one when fishing in obstruction infested waters. Old line gets much weaker in strength when used in sub-zero temperatures. It is wise to spool on fresh line every now and then. Plus, the ice ridges take a heavy toll on monofilament line. Check the line often.

Leaders are not used unless fishing for northern

pike. The least amount of terminal tackle on the line, the greater chance of successful walleye fishing. The shallow water period calls for the minimum amount of tackle to fish the shallows.

J3   LAKES DURING WINTER; Early Ice
Live Bait Methods

There is a lot of fish in the shallows during the formation of early ice. Baitfish draw walleye during low-light conditions. The walleyes are schooled quite heavily at this time and easy to catch when located. Once a school is located a fisherman must stay in contact with the school. That hole often times becomes a regular producer during both early and late ice. The depth is usually between two and ten feet unless clear ice and water conditions prevail. The darker water lakes will have activity in super shallow water while clear bodies have a greater amount of activity near the break. Live bait fishing is generally more productive than artificials during this time.

An assortment of minnows are used. Your choice will depend on the type of lake; natural forage; and general size of fish pursued. For dark water lakes use chubs, fatheads, and mud-minnows. For clear lakes use spot-tail shiners, golden shiners, lake shiners and small suckers. Frozen smelt, crab tails and perch bellies can be used on any type of lake. These guidelines are not rigid. The minnows are used most successfully when hooked through the back, just behind the dorsal fin. This allows freedom of movement without killing the minnow. The shiners are more apt to die quickly. They are relatively fragile and cannot take much handling.

In some lakes and flowages shad are the most abundant forage fish. Use of gizzard or threadfin shad is common. The shad are almost always taken from the front. If you run your fingers under the shads belly towards its head, you will find sharp fin-like ridges that could stick in a fishes throat making them tough to swallow.

When fishing for numbers of fish, small to medium size bait is best. If you are a hog hunter then large shiners or chubs can produce results. Besides minnows, nightcrawlers, leef worms and red worms are used. And on a very small percentage wax worms, black-eyed susans, and meal worms (occasionally to dress an artificial bait).

Depth control is important. It can be achieved by the choice of sinker weight and other devices such as a bobber and floating jig to keep the minnow off of the bottom. Use a number six or eight hook for most of the minnow fishing. When using large bait, use a larger hook. The sinker should be about twelve inches or more from the hook. Use a light weight, just enough to take the bait to the bottom. Allow the minnow to drag the sinker around. By doing this, you can cover a greater area.

Occasionally, an artificial lure is used and live bait is attached to its hooks. A minnow, piece of minnow or piece of nightcrawler is strung over the treble hooks. It adds scent. Some fishermen have had a lot of luck with it. Simply jig the artificial vigorously and then let it sit. The strike usually occurs when at rest. After setting the hook use your hands to fight the fish. Pull slowly and allow the fish to run while keeping a slight amount of pressure on the line. This will wear the fish out. After the fish tires, bring it towards the hole. Get its head into the hole, lower the gaff, insert it behind the gill cover or chin and lift. Make sure that you are lifting with the gaff and not the line. The line may break and cause you to lose the fish. Pull the fish through the hole in one motion. Don't stop until the fish is completely out.

Live bait has advantages over artificials, particularly when fishing is tough, or fishing in shallow water.

J4   LAKES DURING WINTER; Early Ice
Fishing The Shallows

Fishing the shallows is not restricted to fishing along the shoreline area. It also includes the rock and gravel bars as well as underwater islands that are found in the lake proper.

When fishing in shallow water, the fisherman must be extra careful about noise. Fishermen walking around, drilling holes, and snowmobiling can really put the fish down into a negative mood. Try to be as quiet as possible.

Light is another important factor. Use a hole

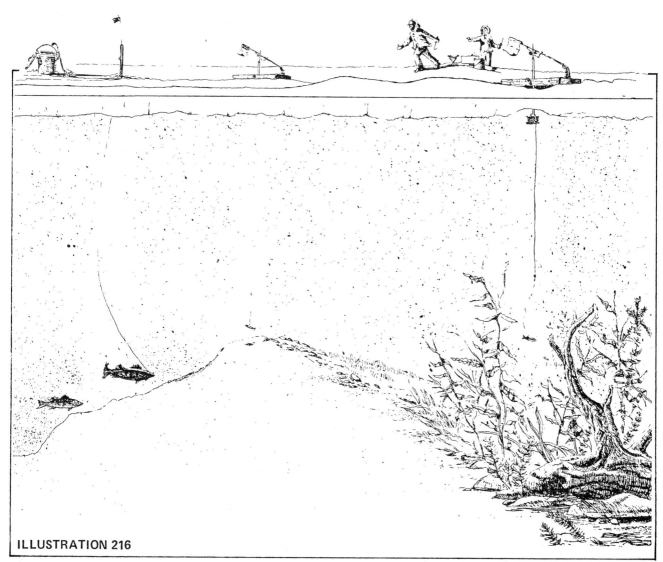

ILLUSTRATION 216

cover wherever tip-ups are placed. The streak of light that is allowed to pass through the hole can keep walleye away from the hole. Clear ice areas have the same effect. The early ice will allow a substantial amount of light through it. Use some of the snow, that can be found in the area, to lightly cover the spot that you are fishing in. When you are finished, gather the snow into one pile. The snow cover stops the light from reaching the vegetation, and it needs all the light it can get. Build some snow up around the hole, this helps to cut down on the light. When finding a productive hole keep working it because they seem to continue to be hot spots throughout the thin ice periods.

To catch walleye consistently, a depth pattern must be established. To start with, string out your tip-ups. Set one shallow *(Illustration 216)* in the weeds or gravel (hole 1). The second one should be at the top of the dropoff (hole 2), and the third should be right off of the drop off (hole 3). If your state only allows one or two tip-ups, start from the shallow water, and work deeper. Move the tip-ups every hour. If one hole starts to produce, move the other tip-ups to that depth. The deeper hole can be jigged. Shallow holes should be worked with live bait.

During the summer, long flats with good structure become hot spots. During the winter, areas that have fast breaks and good structure, and are near to summer hot-spots usually become productive areas. *Illustration 217* points this out. Area

(A) is a weedbed. The fast break has gravel on it. It would be wise to set a tip-up at numbers (1), (2) and (3), to establish depth. It could be productive because it is in proximity to the summer hot-spot and most likely holds bait fish during early ice. The same goes for area (B). Numbers (1) and (2) are set on a small stretch of gravel between the weeds. The weeds offer food and cover.

If none of the tip-ups produce within four hours (that is including moving them around), then string the tip-ups along the break on the shallow water side, in the weeds. Get the percentages going for you. The walleyes will usually move into shallow water during early ice. Not all of them, but a good percentage of them.

K1   LAKES DURING WINTER; Hard Winter Breakline Fishing

The breakline plays an important role in fishing all year long. Walleyes must cross it to get to shallow water. They will use it as a holding area, and move along it when relocating. A walleye that is active and moving around is one that can usually be enticed to accept an offering. Certain spots along the breakline are used more than others. A slight inward or outward dip may be a holding area. It is essential to have good structure located on the break. A build up of rock will draw walleye when baitfish are present. The rocks will offer a point-of-attack when pursuing minnows. Gravel

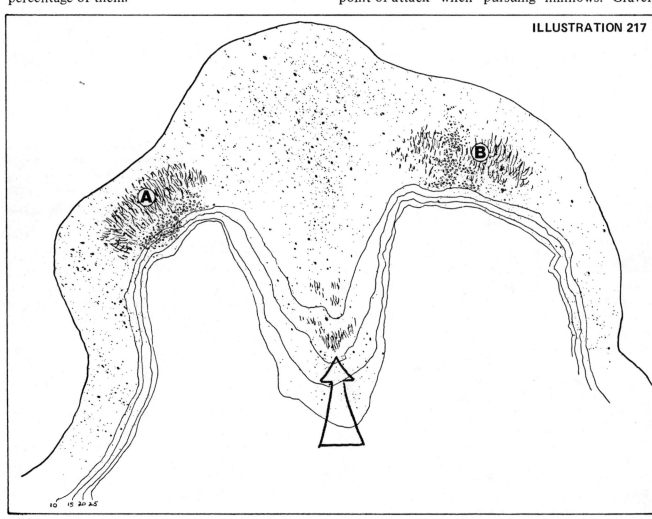

ILLUSTRATION 217

usually harbors aquatic insects, drawing both bait-fish and walleye. The layout of the break is important also. During the summer months, long slopes with adequate structure is the key. During cold water periods, steep breaks that come out of deep water become the better spots.

When a steep breakline is fished, four areas should be covered thoroughly *(Illustration 218):*

AREA I. This is the "skinny" water, or the top of the break. When fish move into shallow water, movement is usually vertical, then horizontal moving towards shore. This cuts down the fishing potential unless accompanied by a weedline or timber. The area of actual movement is small because the walleye heads in towards cover.

AREA II. Walleyes may hold anywhere on the break. This has a greater amount of potential because movement can also be horizontal along the break. Occasionally walleyes will suspend tightly against the break. It is a transferring area because of movements into the shallows.

AREA III. This has the greatest potential for horizontal movement. The base of the break offers the security of deep water and will be used when relocating along the break. Plus it is easy to fish.

AREA IV. This area is seldom explored by the walleye fisherman. However, it has potential, especially when the baitfish move out to deeper waters. Walleyes suspend usually just under the schools of minnows, white bass, crappie and bluegills. Plus walleyes that are spooked off of the break may move out and suspend off of the break.

As the hard winter progresses, movement into deeper water occurs. The walleyes also have a tendency to suspend off the bottom. This is the reason for tough fishing during the mid-winter stage. Admittedly, low oxygen levels and a slower metabolism also effects the walleye.

K2 LAKES DURING WINTER; Hard Winter
Suspended Fish

There are more suspended walleyes caught in winter than summer. The reason is depth control. It is much easier to set at a prescribed depth with tip-ups than trolling at precise depths. The dis-advantages are in the rate of retrieve. The only rate of retrieve in ice fishing is controlled vertical jigging.

When walleye fishing becomes tough during the hard winter months, set your tip-ups at five foot intervals starting from the bottom. Bottom feeding walleyes may be as deep as forty or fifty feet. Stay in relationship to areas that are walleye hotspots during other times of the year, but move deeper. For suspended walleyes, locate the bait-fish and vary the depth from five feet below them to a couple of feet above them. After catching a fish, continue to fish at that depth level. Location of the baitfish is important.

K3 LAKES DURING WINTER; Hard Winter
The Importance Of Baitfish

The baitfish movements and rate of growth is something most walleye fishermen don't pay too much attention to. To get a clear picture of walleye movements you must pay attention to the bait-fish. For instance, perch are a prime food for bottom feeding walleye, both the migratory and weed walleye. During winter, the large perch (desirable size for walleye) move into deeper waters. Young-of-the-year perch stay in the shallows, particularly in weed areas. Whenever you have a split in the food base, you will have a split in location of walleyes.

Crappies and bluegills slowly migrate to deeper water after the thin ice period. After a time, they are caught while suspended over deep water. The white bass move out as do the golden shiners and lake shiners. The split between shallow and deep water forage may be as follows:

EARLY ICE

DEEP WATER	*SHALLOW WATER*
Large baitfish 10%	90%
Small baitfish 10%	90%
Suspended forage 30%	70%

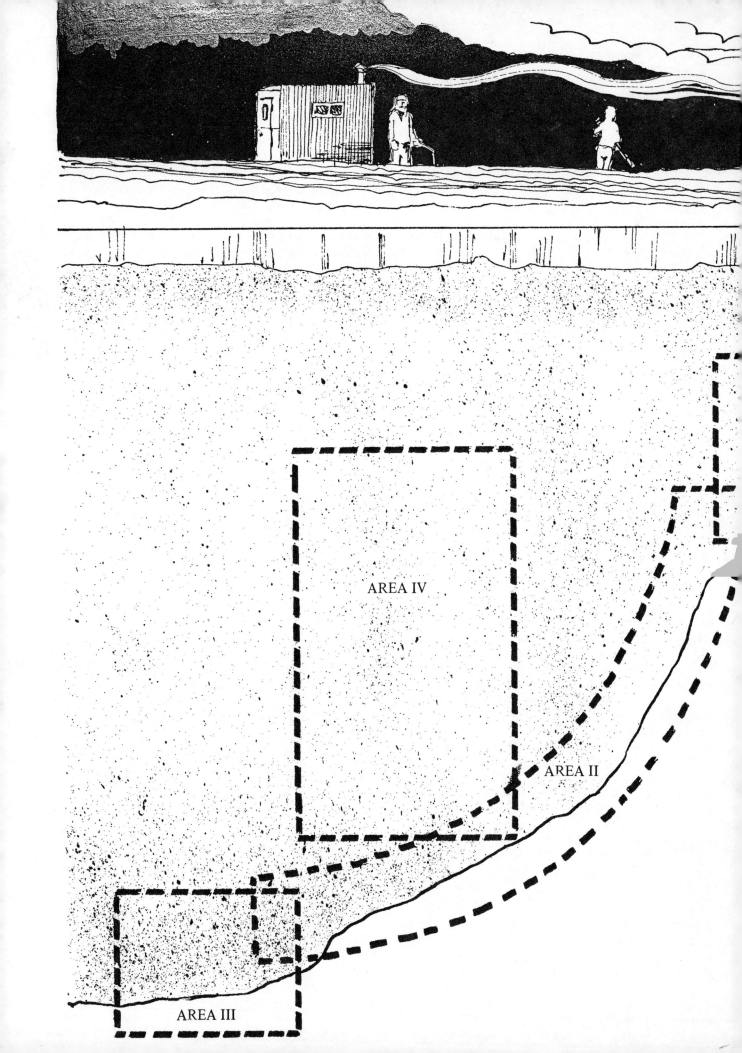

AREA IV

AREA II

AREA III

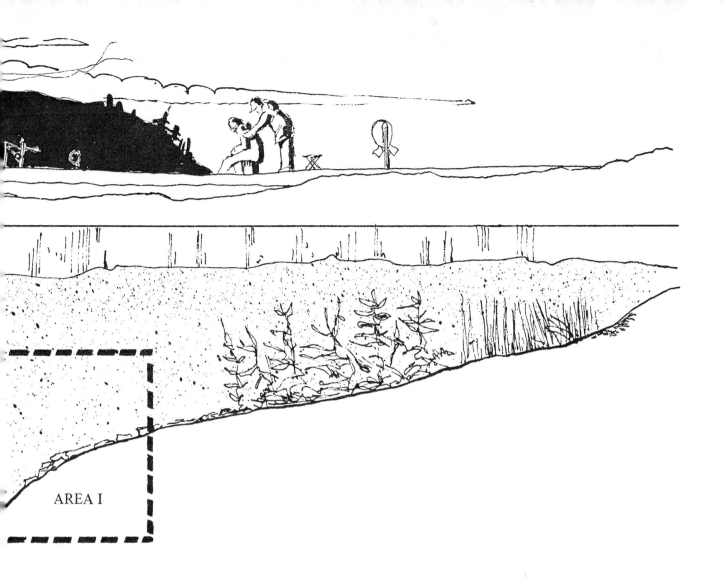

AREA I

ILLUSTRATION 218

AREA I – "Skinny" water. This area is good when walleyes occupy the shallow water, at times they will co-exist with other species and at times are forced to the weed-edge.

AREA II – Holding and vertical movement: Over an extended period of time, is usually associated with a steep break.

AREA III – When relocating (relating to a breakline fish): The base of the structure is used.

AREA IV -- Suspended walleyes are common.
The reason for suspending will, in most cases, determine whether the fish is active or not. If the walleye is spooked into suspending, it will be difficult to catch. If the walleye is suspended because of its relationship to food, it will be easier to catch.

MID-WINTER

DEEP WATER	SHALLOW WATER
Large baitfish 75%	25%
Small baitfish 20%	80%
Suspended forage 90%	10%

LATE ICE

DEEP WATER	SHALLOW WATER
Large Baitfish 10%	90%
Small Baitfish 10%	90%
Suspended forage 40%	60%

These are estimates, and vary from lake to lake. Analyzing this from a practical point of view tells us where the walleyes are going to be. The vast majority of the walleyes will relate to the abundant food base. Others will relate to the smaller percentage areas. Plus each group of walleyes will find and relate to its most desirable food size.

Locating baitfish under the ice is difficult. Locating perch, crappie and bluegill can be accomplished by trial and error while fishing for them, but suspended forage like cisco, shad, and shiners is harder. Having a depth finder is essential. The suspended forage will light up the screen when found. Move out to deeper water off of steep breaks. Pour a little water or anti-freeze on the ice and press the transducer to it. Keep searching til baitfish are located. Bore out a hole and start fishing.

K4 LAKES DURING WINTER; Hard Winter
Live Bait Methods

Still-fishing methods discussed in other chapters will work while ice fishing also. Walleyes will not be very active because of their low metabolism and possibly low oxygen content in the water. The oxygen content is greatly reduced when a hard winter leaves a lot of snow on the ice. The snow stops the light from entering the water. The result is, vegetation begins to die. This plus decaying matter on the lake bottom steals life supporting oxygen. In extreme cases, it causes winter-kill.

With the possibility of low oxygen levels and slow metabolism, walleyes are somewhat sluggish (not in all lakes, some have supporting springs) and harder to catch. Now add the abundant forage fish populations and you can see why fishing is extremely difficult on some lakes during mid-winter.

Live bait is the route to go during tough conditions. There are four basic ways to fish with live bait (Illustration 219). The drop sinker rig is easy to put together (Fig.1). The line from the rod or tip-up is attached to one end of a barrel swivel. Another line is tied to a bell sinker on one end, and the same side of the barrel swivel on the other. Next, a snell is added to the other end of the barrel swivel. Hook the minnow through the mouth or back and you are all set. Lower the rig to the desired depth. In Fig. (2) a standard Lindy Floating Rig is used. The slip sinker rests on the bottom. A floating jig keeps the minnow suspended up high. The snell could be lengthened to almost any length. The difference between this one and the drop sinker rig is on this rig the walleye can pull the line through the slip sinker without feeling much weight. The simplest set-up (Fig. 3) is hook, line and split shot sinker. The minnow is hooked through the back and has freedom of movement. It works great for both bottom feeding and suspended walleye. Occasionally a fisherman jigs with a lead-head jig and minnow (Fig. 4). Steady up and down strokes are employed. The walleye usually strikes on the falling of the bait. The minnow is hooked through the head.

The deep water period will last until the ice starts to thin out with warmer weather and rain.

L1 LAKES DURING WINTER; Late Ice
Black Ice

As the weather warms, the ice gets increasingly dangerous. Black and gray spots appear on the ice. Stay away from them. Air bubbles form and the ice gets extremely weak. Some lakes have springs in them, the ice is dark and very thin. A late season snow storm could cover all of the black ice so be careful.

When fishing during the late season, take an ice spud along and poke around the ice that is in front

ILLUSTRATION 219

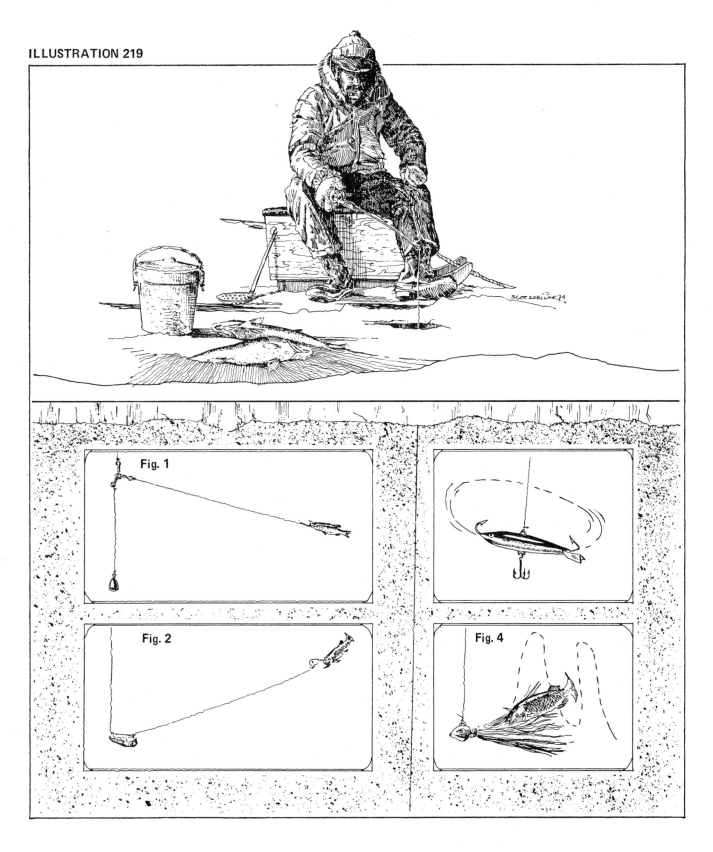

Fig. 1

Fig. 2

Fig. 4

of you. Also make sure that you have a bucket, rope and Coast Guard approved seat cushion.

The best areas for fishing during late ice are near shore. This is a shallow water period. Baitfish and walleyes move into the shallows until ice-out. Fishing can be very productive. Use the same methods previously described for early ice.

L2   LAKES DURING WINTER; Late Ice
The Buddy System

When fishing during early ice and late ice, don't fish alone. Ice fishing does not claim as many victims as open water fishing, but one victim is too many. Fish with at least one other person. When walking on the ice, walk about ten feet apart, a-breast, or one behind the other by approximately the same distance. When fishing together, leave some distance between you. Don't bore holes in a circle and stand in the middle. The body weight of two fishermen could be enough to break through weak ice. Stay away from open water edges.

The buddy system works. Practice doing the little things that I have mentioned . . . you and your buddy might fish together a little longer.

L3   LAKES DURING WINTER; Late Ice
Fishing The Weeds

The type of weeds does not seem to make a difference. The weeds must draw baitfish and the greener the weeds, the better they are. Set the tip-ups near the weed-edge (on the inside edge of the weeds) and work inward towards shore. Walleyes do not school as tightly when in the weeds. If one hole becomes productive, bore other holes near it. The walleyes move in loose schools while infiltrating weeds.

Locate areas that have a weed-edge right at the dropoff. Make sure that the break is steep. The weeds should extend to shore or near it.

Under low light conditions fish shallow because walleyes will move shallow. Under bright light conditions, fish the deeper weeds or in the thicker weeds. The walleyes will really dig in. Light is a negative factor (unless super active). Fishing around sparse weed clumps can be productive when conditions are favorable.

L4   LAKES DURING WINTER; Late Ice
Methods For Locating Fish

If you find the food source, walleyes will be near by. Bore a hole in the shallow water weeds. Take some oatmeal and crackers, grind it up together. Pour a small amount in the hole. If there are baitfish around, they will find the mixture of goodies. Chumming the hole for baitfish is an old trick used in the early days. Don't over do it. Pour in just enough to find out if there are baitfish present. Then send down a minnow, suspended just off of the bottom. Wait about an hour, if nothing happens, bore another hole near to the first one. Don't bait this hole.

Take notice of where the perch and bluegill fishermen are. Often times they gather in groups. Move to the outside of them. Spend a few hours on the outside edge. Often times walleyes will hold just outside of all of the activity.

Fishing near inlets and outlets of lakes is often times productive when the lake fishing is generally poor. But, these are dangerous areas, so be careful. Stay away from the open water and black ice areas.

Moving your tip-ups and jigging rods every hour helps to locate fish. It seems that a newly placed tip-up receives more attention than one that has been sitting for a long while. Also, change minnows often. Try using nightcrawlers, leaf worms and red worms. A walleye will take a variety of baits.

Get a good contour map of the lake and look for spots that are between known summer hot-spots and spawning areas. Resident fish tend to stay in the area.

L5   LAKES DURING WINTER; Late Ice
Cleaning The Area

Included with your ice fishing gear, add a small garbage bag. You can carry your dry gloves in it. Then after fishing, use it for the garbage. It takes a minute or two and the lake will look a lot cleaner if everyone did it.

SECTION III

FISHING THE RIVERS:
SEASON-TO-SEASON

A1   RIVERS DURING SPRING
            The Walleye Run

February and March are known as the "cabin fever" months throughout the upper third of the country. Avid walleye fishermen sharpen their hooks, clean tackle boxes and rearrange their equipment, much like a tidy housekeeper before an expectant party. More and more, conversations lean towards the walleye run. An occasional drive to the river, to check-it-out, rates high on his list of activities. And finally, the walleye run starts!

Resident river walleyes and a great percentage of lake run walleyes (if the river system is connected to a lake) move up the rivers to spawn. Often times a dam becomes the end of the line for these fish. Consequently, fishermen gather near dam sites and fish them. It becomes the concentration site for walleyes.

The run starts when water temperatures increase to approximately forty-two degrees. The males make their way toward prime spawning areas. The males move in relatively large schools — however, they are not necessarily tight schools. The pattern is of the "start-stop" type. They move up to holding areas, mill around, then move again. At their final destination the males move into the shallows at night and to deeper, quieter waters during the day. They will move into the rushing water, or wherever the current offers food, when actively feeding, then drop back behind obstructions to avoid fighting the current.

Meanwhile, the females are slightly aroused to a point of grouping, slowly making their way upstream. Water temperatures must reach the high forties before they are ready to spawn. They will actively feed while moving upstream. Wingdams, boulders, timber and other sorts of obstructions offer both resting and feeding areas. Occasionally the gravel and rock flats, out of the current, provide resting areas as well as nightly feeding areas.

There are ways to check on the early progress of the run. Northern pike spawn before the walleyes do. Therefore, if you are catching some northern and no walleyes, the run has not really started yet. The northern pike action will die off, and a few small male walleyes are caught. This is the start of the run. Weather has a lot to do with the progress of the run. If days are warm and nights mild, the run will continue on course. Freezing nights can slow the run down.

The greatest amount of activity in both feeding and movement is during the night. With the security of darkness, walleyes can move toward the shores trapping minnows as they go. Fishermen dot the river shorelines with lanterns. From the

MISSISSIPPI RIVER walleyes, all caught with jigs, fill up a stringer held by Al Lindner and Gary Roach.

ILLUSTRATION 220

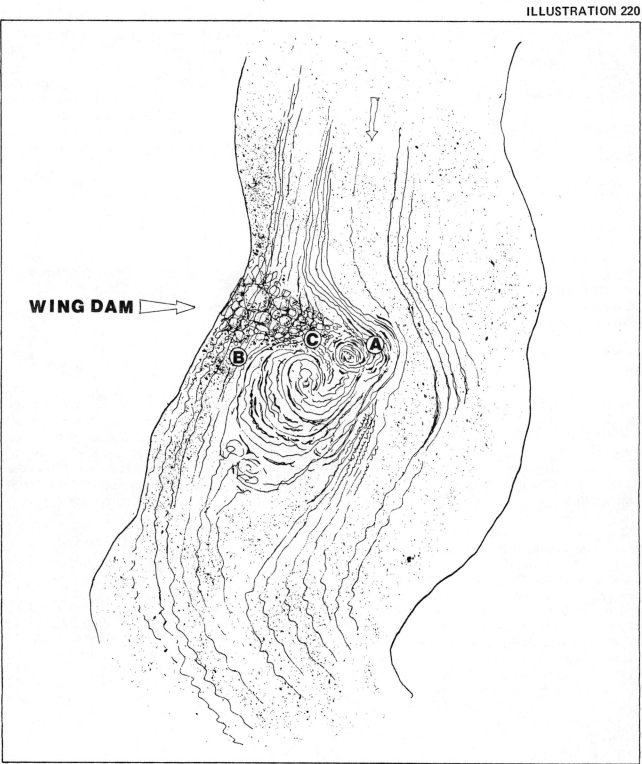

WING DAM

air the dam areas almost look like airport landing fields during the night. Campers are scattered along the well known "hot-spots". Like static electricity there's a feeling of excitement in the air. It's just plain fun to fish during the walleye run.

A2   RIVERS DURING SPRING
Wingdams And Obstructions

Over the years man has tried to alter the course of rivers. A method of funneling water is through the use of wingdams. Some wingdams are natural rock formations that extend out from the shoreline. Man's version is usually a combination of rock, gravel and, at times, timber. The wingdams stretch out from the shoreline, funneling the flow of water downstream. When wingdams and river bed are within a short distance of each other, the wingdam becomes a potential hot-spot. During low water periods *(Illustration 220)* walleyes will use area (A) at the inside edge of the river break (the dropoff that is close to the wingdam). At high water levels they will use area (B), feeding on the shore side and along the down stream side of the wingdam. At normal pool, area (C) is used because the baitfish are also using this area due to strong river currents. The walleye gets into the current long enough to feed (when active), then seeks out holding areas that are near its food. A strong current could "blow" the minnows down stream, so they seek shelter as well.

A true river fisherman knows that if he is not fishing in obstruction infested waters he just is not fishing productively! Obstructions are a problem. You will lose lures, jigs and at times, patience with the whole ordeal. But you must fish these waters to be successful.

Walleyes tend to hold in areas that are behind objects. The slow current flow is created by the presence of the object. Look for the gravel bars behind big boulders; the edge of the current; eddies; the river side edge of the reverse current; and bridge obstructions made of concrete, timber and rocks. Fish on the down stream side of timber, or right in it.

A few years back, some states experienced a severe drought. I often fished on the Rainbow Flowage in northern Wisconsin at the time. The flowage was down to the river bed. Most of the fishermen that I had observed fishing kept casting to the middle of the river bed. That was not productive at all. I casted into the timber laden edges and caught a great number of walleyes, smallmouth and perch. However, I did lose many jigs. There are methods that will cut down on the loss (explained in *Section III, A4)* of lures.

Fishermen gather around the dams because they are the end of the line for river run walleye. It forces them to congregate in one area, making them easier to locate. Few fishermen explore the down stream possibilities. There is great potential wherever there is strong current and current-breaks to offset the speed. Search out these areas and you will find some of your own hot-spots.

A3   RIVERS DURING SPRING
Dams

There are many types of dams. If water flows over the top or through gates that release top water, there is great walleye fishing potential in the area. If the water is released below the dam the greatest fishing potential lies further down stream. An example of this is the Oahe Dam in South Dakota. The water is released well below the depths of the Oahe Reservoir (the body of water

OAHE DAM in South Dakota.

on the upper side of the dam from which the water flows). This cold water is usually around forty degrees or colder. The area just below the dam is too cold for successful spawning. Most of the heavy walleye activity takes place a little further down stream, where the sun can warm up waters in the sloughs. As you can see, the water source is important.

No matter what the size of the dam is, there are certain areas that walleye fishermen concentrate on, depending on the time of day and season. *Illustration 221* is a typical dam.

Figs. (A) and (D) don't have water following down. These gates are shut. In this particular case, (B) and (C) gates are open.

Fig. (E), from one side of the dam to the other is called an "apron". The fast water of the apron rushes over the "lip" (F). Area (G) is a deep washed out hole created by the current. During the night, walleyes move up to the lip, sway back and forth in the current and feed. Occasionally they will move up into the fast current. They do not stay in it for long, dropping back to the lip or hole if they're spooked.

Areas (H) and (I) receive reverse current. At night walleyes will move up into these areas and trap minnows against the walls. If the current is too strong (usually during extreme high water periods), they will drop back to the lip of the hole. During the daylight hours, the hole (G) will hold a great percentage of those night feeding walleyes.

Fig. (J) and (K) are "eddies". The edges of the eddies are good spots. Walleyes move into the saucer-disc like washouts created by permanent eddies during low water periods. The rocks (L) and (N) are used during both high and normal pool periods but strong current will blow the fish right out of there. During a low water period the back side of the washout (O) becomes an area of transference. Walleyes will move to adjoining feeding areas and return to the washout. The wingdam (M) is a super spot. In this case it extends out to the edge of the river bed making it a dynamite holding area. During low water walleyes will move to the tip of the wingdam or in the eddie. During normal pool they will use the length of the wing-

dam, and during high water, walleyes use the shore-line edge of the wingdam all on the down stream side. Timber (P) attracts baitfish, therefore it attracts walleyes. Timber is difficult to fish in, but it is a holding area. If all of the gates were open the shoreline areas with reverse current would be good, also wingdams and obstructions that can hold the fish in strong current. Move down stream to find better current breaks.

A4   RIVERS DURING SPRING
Presentation Methods With Artificials

River fishermen learn the value of the dollar quickly. Losing lures is a fact of life. With common sense and practice one can cut down on his losses. However, expect to lose some baits.

Some modifications can be made to reduce the loss of lures. Take crank-baits for example. Almost all of them have treble hooks attached. When pulled through the water usually one hook hangs down and the other two ride high. Cut the hanging hook off *(Illustration 222, Fig. A)*, it helps to cut down on snags yet does not affect their fish catching ability. Also, use deep divers when working shallow obstructions. The big, long lip acts as a protector and keeps the other hooks from catching every obstruction in sight. At times, I have used the lures in this fashion for several days before losing any. I can't say whether your luck will be as good, but the possibilities are there. And tight action crank-baits hold the hooks closer to the lure than loose action crank-baits.

There are a couple of ways to get around the heavy loss occurred when using jigs. First, there are several jig manufacturers that offer jigs that have weed-guards on them. They are quite effective. *(Fig. B)*. But I find that bending the hook inward with a pliers helps to keep them from getting hung up. You will lose some fish with hook bent inward, however, setting the hook quickly and hard overcomes the problem. It seems that most of the walleyes will be lip-hooked.

Another solution is to purchase jigs with wire hooks as opposed to forged hooks. You must use heavier line when using these jigs. When hung up, put force on the line and the hook will bend and

ILLUSTRATION 221

ILLUSTRATION 222

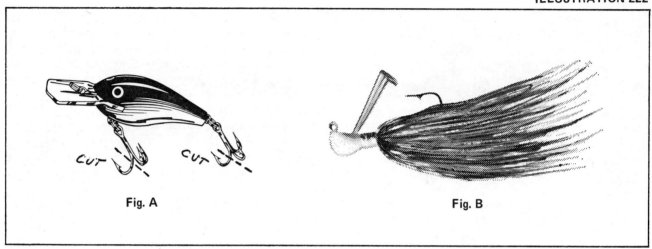

Fig. A   Fig. B

ILLUSTRATION 223

usually release from the obstruction. Set the drag correctly, and you won't have any problems landing a large fish. Set the drag tight enough to get the hook set and loose enough to allow a large fish to pull out line when necessary.

In addition to purchasing jigs with wire hooks, get some cheapies. The six for a buck type. They will lose their head color quickly; chip a little; and maybe even lose their hair, but a lead-head and a hook is all it takes when using a jig dressed with a minnow, leech, or crawler.

Most of the river-rats that I know carry a full tackle box of nothing but jigs in addition to their regular tackle. Jigs for every purpose, plus a large assortment of grubs. The shape of the jig-head is important. Each reacts a little differently in water. *(Illustration 223.)* A round jig-head left to free-fall, tumbles, rolls and turns; but on retrieve it has very short static movements. The wedge-shape lead-head hardly rises or drops on a retrieve, it is quite stable; but left to rest on the bottom, it drops to one side. The swimming head and banana shape lead-head tend to rise in the current. They are excellent choices for a stop and go retrieve. The flat horizontal shape head dives. It is a poor choice for working in the weeds or obstructions. Nevertheless, it is a good lead-head for a straight, mid-water retrieve. The foot-type of lead-head rests upright on the bottom. The hook remains up on an angle. They are becoming very popular for working in weeds. Two nationally known fishermen,

Gapen's Walleye Jig

Banana - Head

Gapen's Horizontal - Head

Spence Petros and Tony Portincaso have developed the power-heads to their fullest potential, using the power-head with plastic attractors (Reapers and Creatures) to catch eye-popping stringers of bass, muskie, northerns and walleyes. The foot-type of jig-head is best used in weeds. Jig-heads that reach the bottom quickly work better because you can pin-point the location that you wish to work. Swimming jig-heads lift in the current and are better for straight retrieves.

There are a number of jig-heads with grubs on the market. They are very good for working the slower water conditions. The Mister Twister Jig and Gapen Grubs are excellent choices. *(Illustration 224)* You can control the rate of descent by choosing the correct weight of jig for the water to be fished and by turning the grub sideways. This adds water resistance to a falling grub and slows it down. At times the slow falling jig triggers walleyes to strike. Knight's Tiny Tube jig is another good one that descends slowly without any manual changes to the lure.

On rivers, do as much vertical jigging as possible. Having control of the lure is essential. When casting, cast up stream and retrieve slowly with the current. Allow the lure to get directly across from you and retrieve it up the reverse current if possible. In this way there is good presentation to the walleyes that are in holding spots in the current and the fish that are at the current break.

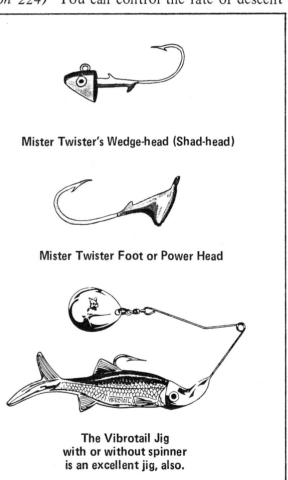

Mister Twister's Wedge-head (Shad-head)

Mister Twister Foot or Power Head

The Vibrotail Jig
with or without spinner
is an excellent jig, also.

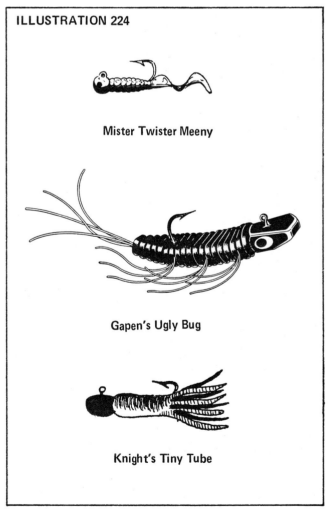

ILLUSTRATION 224

Mister Twister Meeny

Gapen's Ugly Bug

Knight's Tiny Tube

Mister Twister's Sassy Shad jig and spinner combination *(Illustration 225)* works very well when trolled slowly over shallow water or when casting to rock piles. To my surprise (a friend, Tom Meyer, put me onto it) the walleyes really strike at the Sassy Shad. I had thought of it as more of a bass bait, but results don't lie. We have caught a lot of walleyes by trolling the Sassy Shad with spinner in shallow water. I did make one minor adjust-

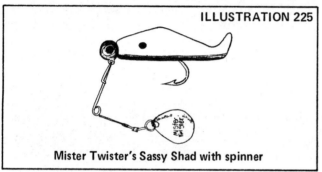

ILLUSTRATION 225

Mister Twister's Sassy Shad with spinner

ment that helped me to boat more fish: adding a treble hook to the rig. Slide the treble hook over the jig hook and stick one of its points into the Sassy Shads back. Less fish are lost to poor hooking.

Another series of lures that are excellent to use on rivers are *(Illustration 226)* the Sonar, Little George and Gapen Slips. They are heavy for their size (usually made of metal), vibrate, and resemble small minnows. You can cast and retrieve them through fast water very easily. They are productive when the walleyes are actively feeding. Some fishermen vertical jig them with success.

Purchase a variety of artificial lures. Get some to cover every depth of water that you might fish. Size and color will depend on the time of year and coloration of the water. During tough conditions move on to live bait methods.

A5   RIVERS DURING SPRING
         Live Bait Methods

At times it may be tough to convince an artificial lure enthusiast that live bait offers another page in lunker-lore. However, live bait is natural in the environment and out-produces artificials when fishing is tough.

One of the problems that a fisherman faces is that he likes to catch fish on his own terms. Often times he uses a bait because he likes using that type of bait; he likes the feeling of the strike on that bait; or he has caught fish on the bait before and has confidence in a particular bait.

Adaptability is the mark of a good fisherman. Personally, I don't like to anchor and fish; but I know that at times I have to . . . or I won't catch anything! Being able to change your style of fishing, your methods and method of attack will increase your chances of becoming a consistent walleye producer. Learn to use the live bait methods.

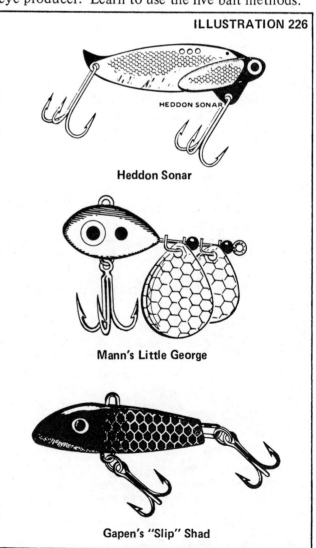

ILLUSTRATION 226

HEDDON SONAR

Heddon Sonar

Mann's Little George

Gapen's "Slip" Shad

The simplest form of live bait fishing includes a bobber, sinker and hook. It is not an attractive method for a veteran fisherman, but it works. Remember, that depth control and presentation is extremely important. At times, the simple set-up will become your ticket to success. It is particularly effective when fishing in heavy obstructions. Cast towards the dam, and let it float down stream. Keep the bait just above the rocks. Cast into the rapids and let the current take the bobber toward the slack water areas. The current will take the bobber to the same areas that it carries the food that the walleye is after. Let the bobber work its way around timber and trees in the water. It is a very unique tool. The sinker should be near the bait, otherwise the bait will rise in the current. Instead of a hook, a jig-head might be used. The length of the rod will determine how deep you can work while retaining the ability to boat the fish. For instance; a seven or eight foot rod allows you to set the bobber at better than six feet from the hook without causing complications when it comes time to land the fish. A short five and a half foot rod requires less line between bobber and hook.

Another solution is to use a water-fillable bobber. With it, one can fill the bobber half-full of water to give it some buoyancy. But, you will lose total depth control.

The actual bait used is determined by season. Minnows work best during spring and fall but can be used all year long (because of the number of baitfish that reside in rivers). Nightcrawlers and leeches work well during summer. If you are in a situation where live bait is tough to get or you run out of it; cut a white strip off of a perch belly and use it. I have caught many walleyes on perch strips.

Leeches are tough. The bluegills and perch won't rob many of them from your hook. They are present in most of our waters and are excellent walleye bait. Leeches are generally nocturnal critters, often found around weeds, timber and gravel. In cold water they curl up into a small ball; dig into the mud; or attach themselves to an object. They have an excellent swimming motion that really attracts fish.

Jigs can be used with any type of live bait. The

RIVER WALLEYES and whitebass caught on Mister Twister Sassy Shads with spinner.

jigs that have been discussed thus far are lead-head jigs. There is another type that is a real asset for river fishermen. It's a "Floating Jig". The head of the jig is made of either cork or a foam plastic. The floating jig is buoyant and floats to the surface if there is no weight attached. Floating jigs are usually used with a sliding sinker or with sinker attached to the line. The jig keeps the bait off of the bottom. Most fishermen try to find a point of buoyancy so the sinker doesn't hang up on every obstruction that lies in its path. The floating jig is very effective. It can be used with any natural bait. It is particularly effective with minnows. The minnow carries the floating jig around as if it had captured some food. A perfect target for a hungry walleye.

The "Wolf-River Rig" which may have other names, depending on your location, is an old standby that has been around for a number of years. It consists of a three way swivel; short line going to a bell sinker; another, but longer line going to a hook; and the third eye of the swivel has the line from your rod attached. The bell sinker is heavy enough to hold in a moderately strong current. The bait swings back and forth in the current. An excellent fish catching tool. There must be current (or it can be trolled) for it to work properly. Any of the natural baits can be used with this rig. Modification of the Wolf-River Rig and others brings us into special river rigs.

A6   RIVERS DURING SPRING
Special River Rigs

Special river rigs were designed to overcome problems and offer specialized methods for fishing in current successfully. The Wolf-River Rig in itself is an excellent tool. However, by adding red beads and a small spinner blade to the snell it is an added attraction. The spinner blade flashes slightly, attracting attention to game fish. It also adds vibration, helping the walleye to locate the bait. The spinner blade should be very small. Red, yellow, copper and chartreuse are good dark river colors, white and silver or chrome are good colors in clear rivers.

Lindy's Flikker Rig has a slip sinker snell with a blade attractor on it. It's very useful in current and when trolling. Attach a minnow, leech or crawler to it. Use the heavier sinker with this rig or leave the slip sinker off and use a keel sinker. This sinker keeps the bait in line, and has less water resistance which helps to keep the bait down. Use the keel sinker with artificials also.

I have used the jig and fly combo very successfully throughout the season on rivers. Thinking that I had discovered something new, I had really gotten excited about it until I noticed some hanging on a sport shop shelf. The setup is simple. Use a fly or small streamer, attach it to the line. Run another line (or the same one) back about twelve

to fourteen inches and attach a jig. You can leave the jig bare or secure a natural bait to it. The walleye usually hits the jig. Once I caught two small walleyes at the same time; one on the fly and one one the jig. This combination works best along a concrete or rocky wall, or when trolling slowly in the current.

In the shoreward regions or fast current (to fish the top water), a sinker attached before a floating lure like the floating Rapala, gets the bait down into the water and forces it to shimmy and flash more. I like to use these lures during spring and fall when there is an astronomical number of bait fish present.

Gapen's Bait-Walker Rigs are great. The Bait-Walker sinker can be worked in rocks and other ob-

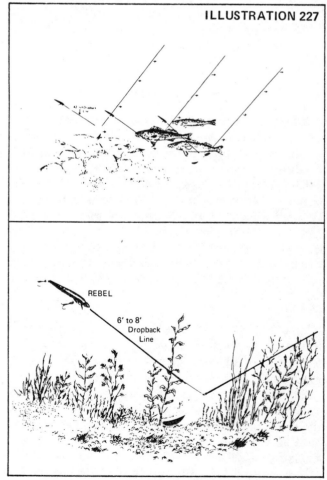

ILLUSTRATION 227

REBEL

6' to 8'
Dropback
Line

structions with a minimum of hang up problems. The Bait-Walker sinker is used with artificial lures for trolling *(Illustration 227)*. The Bait-Walker Snell Rig has an attractor attached which can be used with live bait. The Bait-Walker Float-Rig keeps the bait off of the bottom and is adjustable. And the Bait-Walker Floating Jig Head consists of the trolling sinker, snell and floating jig-head attached. I have found these products to be a notch above the conventional river rigs.

Adaptation is the name of the game. Look over the body of water, figure out where the fish are and pursue your fishing accordingly. If the walleyes are in heavy timber, find a way to get to them. Don't fish an area just because it is easy to fish . . . find the fish, change and experiment with methods that will reach them. Your fishing success depends on it!

A7 RIVERS DURING SPRING
Fishing From Shore

We are fortunate to have great river systems in almost all parts of the country. For boaters and non-boaters alike they offer unlimited fishing potential. Besides, fishing from shore is fun and a great past time. The species of fish that one can catch varies from one river system to another, however, generally there is a wide variety available in each system. And they can be caught from shore.

During spring the most obvious place to fish is near the dams. The walleyes path up stream is blocked by the dam, and therefore the concentration of walleyes is larger there than any other single area. Some states have laws that prevent you from fishing close to the dam, so check on the laws first. If the laws permit, cast towards the dam and work your bait through the white water (rapids). Let it drift past the point where you are standing, then slowly work it back up in the reverse current. Minnows, leeches and nightcrawlers are the best live baits, and minnow imitation lures are the best artificials. Fishing for walleyes can be productive during day and night.

While fishing from shore, the wingdams can be a bit tricky. During low water periods, cast out to the end of the wingdam; during normal pool, fish on the down-stream side, along the rocks and timber; during high water fish very close to shore, at the base of the wingdam. Ninety nine percent of your fishing will be on the down stream side of the wingdam. Occasionally, during a low water period, walleyes will congregate on the up stream side, closer to the tip of the wingdam. Often times it is necessary to use a larger jig, because it is important to get the bait to the base of the wingdam, and as close as possible. The current (when strong) tends to push your bait further down stream when working near the tip. The reverse current moves along the edge of the wingdam and can carry a light weight jig back out into the river current.

Reverse current is interesting fishing water. Walleyes that are feeding usually face the current. So it is advisable to cast down stream in the reverse current and work your lure back up it. There is an area between the reverse current and the river current that is usually slow moving water. Some call it the "slick". This area affords the walleye an opportunity to rest without fighting the river currents. The area is dynamite when it coincides with obstructions such as rocks, boulders, timber, a break and abutments. Sometimes, a single big fish will hold behind an object. Catch the fish and before long another replaces it, because it is a natural holding place.

Bridges along the river offer current breaks at their foundations. The foundations that are nearest to the dropoff are best. Bottle-neck areas sometimes created by the placement of a bridge provide good walleye fishing. Wherever the river narrows, fish movement is concentrated to a smaller area. Walleyes must move through these areas when moving both up stream and down stream. The smaller the area of concentration, the greater the percentage of fish catching potential.

Deep holes in a shallow river are also good for walleye. Often times the rim of the hole is better than the bottom of it (except during fall). The holes are better during low water periods. If the rim has a lot of obstructions, it can be a dynamite spot.

Knowledge of the area is important when fishing

from shore. Get a good river map of the area that you intend to fish. Circle the places on the map where the river bed comes close to the shoreline *(Illustration 228)*. Concentrate your efforts on areas such as (A), (B), and (C). It is not necessary to cast as far into the river as humanly possible. Work the obstructions even if they are within a foot or two from shore.

B1   RIVERS; EARLY SUMMER
Fishing The Current Breaks

A current break is anything that regulates, detours or obstructs the current. The actual form may be a rock, tree, boulder, wingdam, bridge abutment, etc. With proper depth, location and water clarity, they can provide excellent holding areas for walleyes. Obviously the downstream side is the side to fish.

As in lakes, the river run walleye goes through a transitional period where fishing for them becomes tough. Usually this period marks the end of the spring spawning run. Males are the last to be active and finally move out of the spawning areas. Patient fishermen catch an occasional fish along the holding areas. The transition stage lasts much longer in lakes than in rivers. Soon (possibly less than two weeks during warm stable weather) walleyes start showing up on stringers again.

The areas to fish for uncooperative walleyes include slow current breaks down stream from the dams; in the boulder areas where slow current moves through the formations; the deep river bed areas and deep sloughs out of the current. Most of the fish caught will be males. Females are usually deeper. Fish along the steep current breaks and in the river bed.

B2   RIVERS; EARLY SUMMER
Shallow Water Jack Pot

The males are the first to school and return to shallow water patterns. The rock piles and shallow current breaks are very productive. There is a lot of action in the shallow water of the deep sloughs that are connected to the main river channel. Schools of males are on the move providing many

hot and cold fishing areas. A school of males may be in one location for a short period of time and then move, or remain for several days before moving. The fisherman that spends time locating active fish has a better chance of scoring than the fisherman that puts all of his eggs into one basket and marries a spot.

At this time of the year the fisherman can use a wider selection of baits and lures. Minnows such as the river shiner, chub, lake shiner, mud-minnow, and fathead are popular. Also, leeches are widely used, they are common to most river systems and are easy to use. Large, fat, juicy nightcrawlers are in demand.

B3   RIVERS; EARLY SUMMER
Locating Larger Fish

Admittedly, the males will be easier to catch, and locating large females is tough. The reason for the difficulty in locating large females is because of their feeding patterns which are brought on the very nature of river systems. There are times where big fish will be concentrated near the dams and that is during the spawning runs of spring and some of the late fall movements because of the location of their food.

But during the early summer, in medium to shallow water, the big fish tend to take up individual holding spots. A spot that offers a point of attack, cover, and a chance to get out of the force of strong current. Concentration is a result of a prime stretch of such spots in a section of the river. Occasionally, a group of large walleyes will be found on a particular spot, but it is an exception to the rule.

The areas that offer big fish potential (when talking numbers of big fish) are the stretches of river that have these features: a deep river bed associated with timber fields in the shallower water; rocky stretches of the river; areas where the river bed splits into more river beds or where well defined creek channels meet the river; and areas where there is deep water present with many obstructions. Stay away from the long flat stretches of river, unless there is a deep river bed running through it. Fish the rocky points, weeds and con-

ILLUSTRATION 228

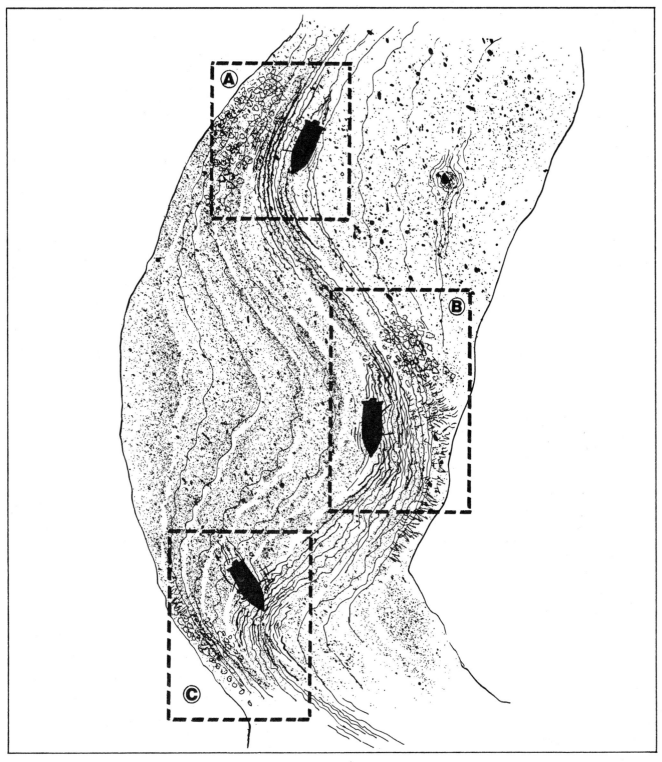

necting river bed areas where the main body of the river widens to almost lake size proportions.

Some of the big fish will remain near dam areas (if there is a large deep wash out) and be quite active at night. During the night the walleyes will move into shallow water, feed and return to the deep hole. The lip of the hole towards the dam is the best spot to fish. Motor trolling to hold the boat in place is by far the best method to overcome the current.

B4   RIVERS; EARLY SUMMER
Trolling, Drifting And Anchoring

The method by which you choose to control your boat will depend on the stretch of river that is to be fished. I have witnessed fishermen dangerously anchored near dams. Use good judgement, do not be blinded by wishful dreams that could turn into nightmares. Safety should be your first priority.

Trolling can be hazardous to your motors health, unless you are very careful when trolling out of the river bed itself. Knowledge of the tell-tale signs of obstructions is important. Usually boils and rippled top water currents are an after-fact of the obstruction. When you see a boiling of the water, the

WITH BAIL OPEN, a back-troller feels the strike with his finger, immediately releases the line to allow the walleye to take the bait without resistance. The bail is then closed to pick up slack line and the hook set.

obstruction is just a few feet upstream of it. A choppy line almost parallel with shore indicates a sharp break. Strong currents push the water upward as other currents move against it. At times the water will be extremely shallow just shore-side of the choppy line.

Forward trolling along the edge of the river bed can be very productive during the early summer period. Heavy weights must be used when fishing in the strong currents of the river. Gapen's Bait-Walker sinker is an excellent choice. Others include the Lindy Slip Sinker, and Twister Rigs. Use these sinkers with either live or artificial baits. Troll slow enough to keep in contact with structure. Forward troll against the current at the edge of the river bed *(Illustration 229, Fig. A)*. When fish contact is established, hover over the area and work it thoroughly.

Back-trolling (developed by Al and Ron Lindner) is particularly effective when the current is mild or slow. Boat control is necessary when working obstructions in the river. Back-troll *(Fig. B)* against the current and along sides of the obstruction, then right over the obstruction if possible. Use live bait or minnow imitation artificials.

Boat control is essential when working on rivers. There are a lot of obstacles involved. Certain areas in rivers are usually full of obstructions. You must fight currents and it seems that the lures snag up on everything in sight. With this in mind, Dan Gapen (lure manufacturer and excellent river fisherman) developed a method, combining boat control and lure presentation, called "Slipping". Slipping is a method of boat control by which the operator moves the boat forward in the current, then puts the motor in neutral and slips backwards, using forward thrust to control the amount of slip. The lure is presented in such a manner that it appears to be fighting the current and dropping back as if losing the battle. After slipping back to a non-productive area, the boat is moved upstream and positioned a little more to the right or left of the obstruction *(Fig. C)* and starts the procedure over again. Both live bait and artificials can be used.

Anchoring on the river can be very effective. Anchoring below a dam could be a "kiss-of-death".

ILLUSTRATION 229

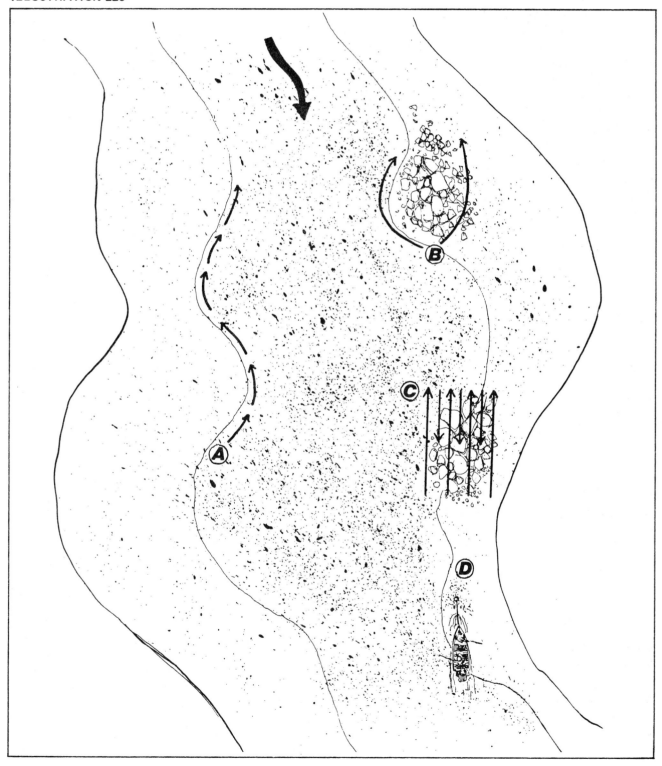

GRAVEL STRETCHES on shore frequently continue into the water. At night walleyes move up to such structure to feed on minnows and aquatic insects. Look for these areas by day and make sure to be there at sundown.

I know of a fellow that anchored below a dam (he had a small pram). The current became stronger and waves started to come over the front of his boat. The anchor would not release. Luckily, he had a knife handy and cut the rope. That knife probably saved his life.

When anchoring use one anchor off the bow of the boat. By doing it this way *(Fig. D)* the boat swings back and forth allowing you to vertical jig an area effectively. Try to anchor in places that offer a variety of structural difference and depth within the area that the boat swings.

The time of day makes a difference also. Walleyes will be active closer to the deeper water during the day on a clear water river. At night a percentage of them will move into the shallow water obstructions. On dingy colored rivers, they can be active at almost anytime. Again a certain percentage of the walleyes do move into the shallower water. The problem is that the obstructions are difficult to fish at night because you can't see them, and a light will spook the walleyes. Spot-casting with live bait or artificial lures will work if you know the area. It is better to work for the walleyes that may come up to the tops of the rock shoals and wingdams.

Some rivers are not open to motor trolling. To cover a lot of water you must drift. Drifting is fine when it is controlled. Use your outboard motor for steering. Try to drift over the prospective fishing areas with a watchful eye. When reaching the end of a bar, motor up it and drift back down another portion of it. Use drifting as a means to fish with a purpose.

B5   RIVERS; EARLY SUMMER
Spot-Casting

Spot-casting is casting with a purpose, casting with the knowledge of what you are casting at. This could be an obstruction, the break, a weed line, the edge of a rock shoal, etc. Spot-casting can be accomplished from shore or from a boat. Find out where the wingdam is and cast to the upstream edge of it, bringing the bait to the productive side. Cast to the base of standing trees near the river bed.

During the early summer period the obstructions that lead into the shallows from the deep river bed are best. Also rock or gravel mounds serve as feeding areas for the walleye. The obstruction must break the current and have a slope of gravel or broken rock behind it. Shallow water fishing is pretty good during this time of the year.

B6   RIVERS; EARLY SUMMER
Day Or Night

Some rivers are very clear like the Missouri River in the Dakota's. Others such as the Mississippi are darker waters, while the St. Lawrence River is more of a medium colored river. The time of year makes a difference also. During spring, the spring run-off causes rivers to get muddy and dark. There is more night movement of walleyes in the clearer rivers because the cover of darkness allows the walleyes to move shallow. During the day, these clear rivers force the walleyes to seek cover in and around obstructions and in deeper waters. On the medium to dark colored rivers some shallow movement takes place even during the mid-noon of day. And during the night some walleyes move into obstructions such as timber and stumps. Needless to say, they are very difficult to catch. Fishing in the weeds at night, in slack water areas, can be productive. Usually a few big fish will be taken each year from these areas. The reason more are not taken is because of the lack of fishing pressure.

The early summer period provides an excellent opportunity to catch some walleyes at night. The shallow water population increases because of two reasons: resident shallow water fish are active and migrating walleyes move into the shallows during the early summer period. Skimming as described in *Section II, E7,* is a particularly effective method of taking walleyes at night. Also live bait cast to the shallows and worked very slowly in the weed clumps pays off.

Lures for river fishing? I like to use crank-baits along the weed edge or river breakline; floating artificials, such as the Rapala, in shallow water obstructions; a jig and minnow on the deeper breaks and some gravel areas; and live bait rigs when trolling slowly . . . during both day and night.

C1   RIVERS; LATE SUMMER
Deep River Breaks

The summer seems to pass by so quickly. The easy walleyes diminish to an occasional good catch here and there. Unlike lakes where a great percentage of the walleye population heads for deeper waters, the walleye population thins out over the river system with some fish moving to deeper water. The fisherman must accurately choose the structures that might hold some fish. The dam areas (if there is sufficient deep water nearby) will always hold some walleyes. It is a natural feeding grounds for gamefish. Nevertheless, a smart fisherman will

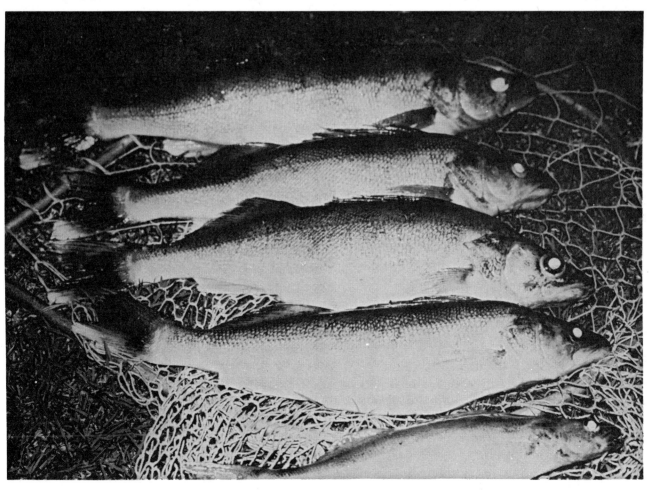

ILLUSTRATION 230

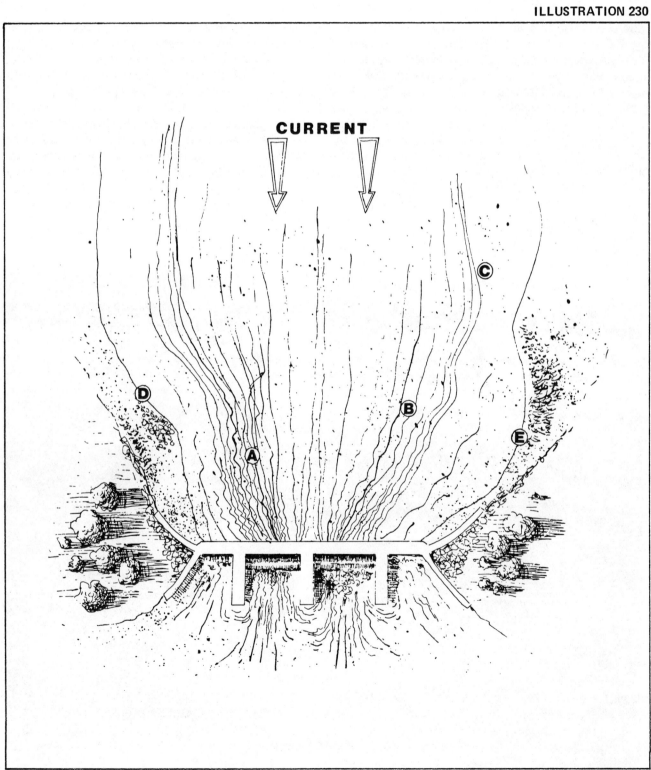

CURRENT

move downstream and mark off the river channel with marker buoys. Fishing the dropoff (break) of the river channel is usually productive. Find the points along the break and spend some time on each.

Locate the areas where river channels meet with other river channels or a creek arm that extends out into the river. Fish the bottom of the break and river channel along the edges. Look for channels that go into large sloughs. Fish around the obstructions that are nearest to the main channels. A flat that comes off of the main river bed can be very productive if the flat has a lot of holding spots on it. The holding spots may be weed clumps, rocks, boulders or timber.

Generally an area that has been productive will continue to be so until there is a major change in weather, or the food that the walleye is feeding on moves. Then it is time to relocate, and find other productive areas.

Movement of walleyes in a river system is a fact of life. You can experience terrific fishing one day and the next day might leave you empty handed. Having five or ten good spots will help. Don't over fish the spot. Take a few fish and move on to another spot. If you do this, you will have a greater number of long lasting productive spots.

C2   RIVERS; LATE SUMMER
Movement Towards The Dams

As summer progresses, there is a noticeable movement towards the dams. Not the headwater dams, like in early spring, but the tailwater dams . . . particularly the deep water above the dam. Walleyes are scattered throughout the river system. However, when the walleyes seem to disappear, there is a decent population of them in deep water, at the dams. A reasonable explanation is: the baitfish start to descend to deeper water as the summer progresses. The baitfish move to deep pools and the deep area near the dams during late summer. Others move into the shallow timber, weeds, and rock areas. Consequently some shallow water walleyes remain, while others follow the deep forage.

The best areas to fish are *(Illustration 230, Fig.1)* along the base of the breaks. Frequently when feeding the walleyes move to shallower breaks, feed, then return to deeper water. Breaks (A) and (B) are the deeper breaks most often used. Breaks (C), (D) and (E) are used when the conditions are favorable (low-light conditions).

The deep water methods mentioned for lakes will work here also. Lindy Riggin' along the break should produce some fish. If not, work the river bed using a longer snell (possibly four or five feet). There aren't many fishermen that work the deep water near the dam. The action is relatively slow, but some good fish are taken. Walleyes are starting to get heavy now. The fish that had been a pound and a half a month ago are now pushing two to two and a half pounds.

THIS SHALLOW WATER WALLEYE was taken from the river near obstructions where it found both food and cover.

C3   RIVERS; LATE SUMMER
Special Problems

The shallow water walleye moves into the heavy obstructions in the shallows. The problems of shallow water fishing are hard to overcome. Rocks, weeds and timber claim their share of lures on the river. I have some tips that will save some lures for you.

Try to fish with a straight line when trolling slowly through the obstructions. When hung up, just move back a little and work the lure loose. Give the line a little slack while backing over the object. Some fishermen keep a taut line, and the result is a broken line.

When using crank baits, cut off the dangling hooks. The other two shanks of the treble hook should ride upwards. A long lip on the deep diving crankbaits helps it to maneuver over obstructions even though using it in shallow water.

When fishing weeds with artificial lures, use floaters. Work the lure above the weeds. It is particularly effective at night and under other low-light periods. An imitation minnow works best.

A simple bobber, snell and hook with a minnow is the answer for shallow water weeds and tree limbs. The current will take this set-up through without any trouble at all. When hung up, just shake the tip of the rod . . . usually it will work its way out of a jam.

C4   RIVERS; LATE SUMMER
Back Water Breaks, Resident Fish

Almost all of the larger river systems have back waters that are quite deep. Some appear to be lakes, except for the fact that they connect to the main body of the river and are regulated by the dam. Generally, rising water means good fishing (high water is tough), and falling water seems to turn them off. When the water is lowered during the latter part of summer, most of the walleyes move back into the main river body. But, some resident fish remain if there is deep water present.

The resident fish will remain in the back waters as long as food and cover is present. Current us-

ually takes care of oxygen problems. The resident fish almost act like lake fish. Except when there is a strong current in the main body, many baitfish move into the back waters. This provides an excellent food base. So, when the gates are open, fishing below the dam and the back waters improves.

As soon as the gates are closed, fishing is a little tougher, unless the wind moves the top water (and builds up water) into the back water areas. It is not uncommon to have the river current flowing one way, and the wind moving the top water in the opposite direction. For the back waters this can mean a movement of baitfish. As the wind subsides, the build up of top water flows with the current causing a slight rise in the water level . . . downstream. This provides additional good fishing for a short time.

When walleyes move from the back waters to the main body due to a lack of food or low water conditions, they will usually move to the points or other good structure in the main body but connected with the back water section. These same areas are good holding spots for river-run walleyes that may be on the move toward the dam areas. Outline the points with marker buoys and work them.

C5   RIVERS; LATE SUMMER
Mapping It

River systems should be plotted just as one would plot out a lake. Marker buoys are very important because current is deceiving. It is very easy to drift off of a spot and not even realize it. The edge of the river bed should be fished during the late summer period. Marking the deeper water current breaks that the dropoff has to offer is essential.

In *Illustration 231, Fig. 1,* (A) represents a slight current break and provides a holding spot for walleyes. Location (B) is particularly good because it is the edge of the river bed and receives water movement to and from the back water bay (E). At the back water side of (B) there will be a reverse current and possibly an eddy if the current is strong. Walleyes that move out of the back water

ILLUSTRATION 231

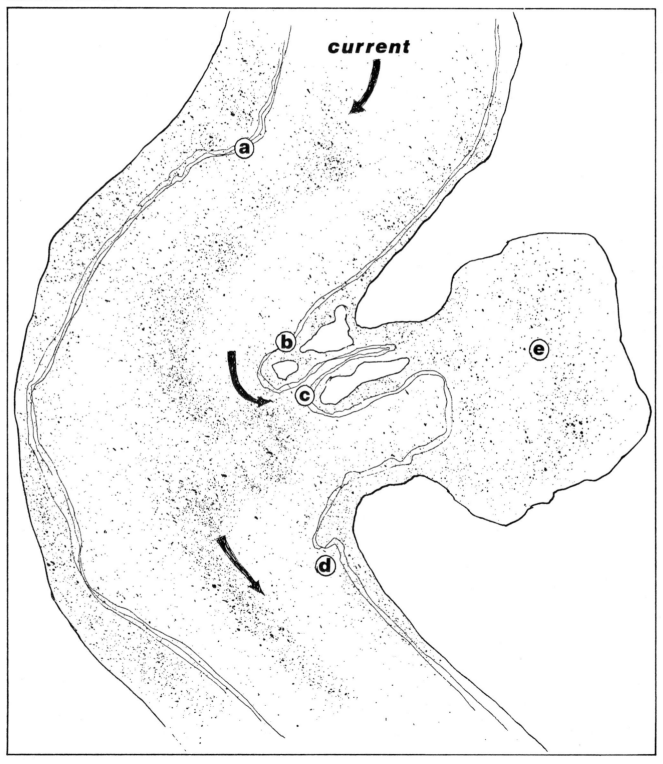

ILLUSTRATION 232

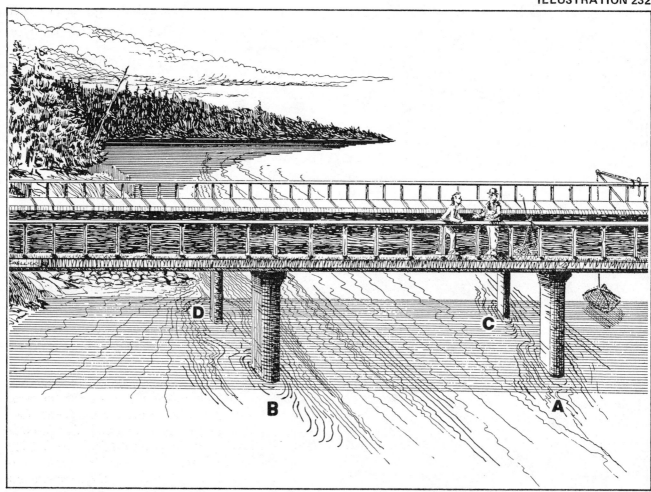

bay may use (B) or (C) as a holding area. It is a good current break and if the bar has rock or timber on it, it will provide food and shelter for baitfish. The small finger (D) could be a dynamite spot when the top water moves in the same direction as the river current. It will provide a current break for minnows that are blown down stream by the strong currents. These spots are typical of the type you should be looking for.

Get a good contour map of the river system or portion that you are going to fish. Take a colored pencil or pen and mark all of the points and areas along the river bed that look like they will provide shelter from the current. Be especially concerned about areas that connect with other river beds, creek arms and deep back water bays.

After completing the homework, motor along the areas that you have marked. Look for additional ones that aren't on the map. These may turn out to be new hot-spots. The idea is to find many current breaks that are close to each other. The ones on the map and the ones you find on your own. This sets up the potential for movement from one to another and is close-by for the walleyes. While fishing you may unintentionally draw a school of walleye off of a current break and they will move to another, usually one that is near by.

Another way of finding good breaks is with the use of your locator to hunt around for baitfish. Move around various structures, look for suspended baitfish and notice how they are relating to the structure. They may be using the inside turn of a finger, or the downstream side of a point, or maybe hanging off of a flat. Fish along the sides of the structure that shows signs of baitfish being present. Mapping and using markers to plot out an area is wise and usually results in a more productive fishing trip.

D1 RIVERS; THE FALL RUN
Returning To The Dams

As summer draws to an end, walleyes move up in to the shallows for a brief period of time. Rock islands, weed bars and other good structured areas become temporary hot-spots. it may be that cool nights trigger movements, combined with baitfish movement into shallow water. Whatever the reason, this feeding spree is short, usually lasting just over a week. It usually takes place during early September in the upper third of the country.

Then as quick as it started, fishing slows down. The slow down lasts until a couple of cold weather weeks have passed. Water temperatures cool off to the high forties. The walleye action picks up as they move toward the dam areas. The entire walleye population does not move toward the dam, but a great percentage seems to. The run and shallow water movements is at its peak when water

PLOTTING OUT a river point with markers, Tom Meyer will fish the shallow side first.

temperatures drop and hold in the mid-forties. This shallow water movement lasts until ice-up in most areas.

There are a couple of reasons for the movement. One is, fall spawning baitfish head for the dam areas during late fall. The walleye follows its quarry. The dams provide an excellent food shelf, and minnows are often times trapped, setting up a point of attack for the walleye. Some fishermen believe that some walleye remain near the dam area until they spawn in spring. I believe that some do.

The run in itself is very much like the spring run. The males are abundant and are found in the same type of holding areas as in spring. A fisherman can fish from shore or a boat and be productive. That is what is nice about these runs. You can stop on the way home from work, or while traveling with the family. It is a pleasant way to spend a few hours.

D2 RIVERS; THE FALL RUN
Fishing Abutments

Fishing along the abutments can be productive, if they are the only means of structure in the area. The rocks along the shoreline are excellent also, and better during low-light periods. The foundation of bridges alter the current *(Illustration 232)* enough to create current breaks and sometimes eddies. The walleyes will hold on the downstream side of the foundation. With fish holding in (A), (B), (C) and (D), the cast must be made to the area ahead of the pillar. Let the bait ride in the current by lifting your rod tip. Give the bait some slack when it reaches the prospective fish holding area. Let it sit for a few moments, then retrieve slowly. The best pillars are just above the river bed drop-off.

The rock and gravel shorelines of the bridge areas are good. Crayfish find the rocks inviting. Minnows of different varieties use the rocks as protection against the current and predators. Walleyes mill around the gravel areas at night, in search of food. During the day, they drop back into a little deeper water.

Some of the old railroad bridges have massive timber piles that support them. The old pilings are catch-alls for aquatic insects of all types. In turn baitfish relish these areas, so much that some remain there all year long. Some of the old bridges have been dismantled but most of the pilings remain. Walleyes and smallmouth bass relate to the pilings often. The current break may not be visible, but most of the navigational maps point them out.

D3   RIVERS; THE FALL RUN
                    Obstructions

When thinking of obstructions most of us picture rocks, weeds, and timber. Typical structure that is found in lakes and rivers. There are other forms that we overlook. Some of them are wrecks, old foundations, fish cribs, etc. Rivers when altered by man usually create flowages and reservoirs. Some of the areas are flooded leaving man-made foundations. Some charts show where the old school house was, where roads once were (and still are); where the quarrys were, etc. The deeper foundations are used during the summer period, but shallow water structures that lead to the dam areas become hot-spots during the fall run. These foundations gather baitfish, and in turn are used by the walleye.

Get a good navigational chart of the prospective fishing area. They show areas in detail that can turn out to be some of your best spots. If a map is not available, ask local residents of the dam area. They will be most involved with the project and probably have some answers for you. Ask about the original river bed, when it was flooded, if buildings were present, are there any man-made structures present, etc. Do a little research. It pays off.

D4   RIVERS; THE FALL RUN
                Jigging Your Way To Success

Most river fishermen will agree. If given one lure to use for the rest of your life on river systems, the answer would be a jig. Jigs are versatile. They can be effectively used in all depths of water, with any form of live bait, are not expensive and anyone can learn how to use them within minutes. With jigs there isn't a right or wrong way to use them; it's a matter of which way works best at the given situation.

Jigs are available in many different sizes, shapes, colors and with or without hair or plastic bodies. (More on jigs in *Section II, (A4).*) The color of the jig depends on the color of water to be fished. Generally speaking, a light color jig for clear water, and a dark color jig for dark water. The most popular colors for rivers are black (can be used anywhere), yellow, and white.

There are some basic methods of retrieve, then your own adaptations can be added:

The swim retrieve: cast the jig, as soon as it hits the water, count 1001, 1002, 1003, etc. (the average rate of descent is one foot per second). When the depth of retrieve is achieved, reel the jig slowly, lifting your rod slightly as it comes. When reaching a one o'clock position with your rod, drop the tip back down to three o'clock and take up the slack, slowly. Most fishermen measure depth with the first cast, counting until the jig hits the bottom. On subsequent casts, the jig is allowed to sink approximately three feet off of the bottom.

The drag retrieve: recommended for sand flats. If used in obstructions you will lose a lot of jigs. Cast the jig, let it fall to the sand bottom. Hold your rod at a three o'clock position. Crank the reel handle very slowly, keeping the line taut. Drag it all the way back to the boat. The strike is difficult to feel unless the walleyes are really active. Most of the time there will be a feeling of added weight; occasionally you will feel a tap. Either way, set the hook fast and hard.

The jigging retrieve: this one is simple and productive. Cast the jig, letting it settle to the bottom. With moderate speed, lift the rod to the one o'clock position. Then lower the rod to three o'clock and take up the slack line while lowering the rod. Do this in a continuous motion until fully retrieved. The strike usually occurs while the jig is falling.

The snap retrieve: this retrieve is effective when the walleyes are active, but under tough conditions I would not recommend it. Cast the jig and let it fall to the bottom. Lower the rod tip to three o'clock. Using your wrist, snap the rod lightly.

terpreted with a shorter line. If you can't feel the strike, you will never know whether you have had one or not.

The jig is a tool that is used for mapping the bottom of the lake.

When dragging the jig through sand, the feeling is tacky. A drag and sudden release sensation is felt. When in soft mud, a continuous drag is felt. When worked over a gravel bar, it feels like many short strikes or taps. Many fishermen think that they are hits and set the hook frequently. When retrieving over rocks, an occasional hard tap is felt. You can also tell whether the bottom is flat, bumpy, or covered with debris.

Small jigs are used with bobbers in the fast water areas where walleye may occasionally feed. The bobber also provides relatively safe passage around obstructions.

When vertical jigging from a boat, the speed of descent is important. Position the boat over the prospective fishing spot. Lower the rig to the bottom, snap your wrist bringing the rod tip to about two o'clock. The descent is the critical part of jigging. Keep a taut line and slowly lower the jig back down to the bottom. When fishing to an active school, the rate of descent can be fast, but in most cases, lower it slowly. Try to jig vertically. This gives you a position of instant contact and response.

The jig and minnow combination is about the most productive way to use a jig. It's deadly and will help you to jig your way to success.

A TEN-POUND FALL WALLEYE taken by Dave Csanda on the Mississippi.

The snap should not move the rod tip more than six inches. Lower the rod tip and do it again. The retrieve takes a long time to complete, but can be effective. The strike usually occurs right after the snap. Allow a second or two between snaps.

By using combinations of these basic patterns, you can create your own retrieves. Remember these principles: the colder the water the slower the retrieve; use the lightest weight that you can use and still maintain contact with the bottom; and short casts are effective. Unless there is a particular reason for an extremely long cast, don't do it. The messages felt through the line are better in-

D5   RIVERS; THE FALL RUN
Special Techniques

Most of the lures on the market were designed to overcome problems that the everyday fisherman faces. From there, the frills were added to sell lures (fishermen buy lures, fish don't). And whenever a manufacturer finds success with a lure, it is copied by others. Some are poor quality and others are improvements on the originals. We as fishermen do the same thing. We purchase a lure and often times make adjustments to fit our particular situation. There's nothing wrong with that.

Take a Lindy Rig for example. The Lindy Rig straight out of the package will do the job for most situations. It's an excellent rig. Occasionally, the fisherman needs a longer snell and adds his own five or six foot snell. The adaptation allows the bait to suspend higher in the water. At times walleyes are suspended well off of the bottom, especially when actively feeding in rapid water. A small cork added to the snell helps to suspend the bait in current.

When frequent adjustment of the sinker distance from the hook is needed, use a rubber band as a stopper. Take a small piece of rubber band and tie it to the line in between the hook and slip sinker. Tie it tightly, it won't cut the line. Now slide the rubber band up the line to whatever distance is desired. It will temporarily stop the sinker from sliding down to the hook. Don't forget to trim the ends of the rubber band. This will give you enough time to find out whether a prospective depth is productive.

Adding a stinger hook to a jig is simple, helps to keep the minnow on, and adds to the number of fish on the stringer. Take a short but strong piece of monofilament line, tie one end to the jig hook or eye. Tie the other end to a small treble hook. Insert one of the treble hooks points into the under-side of the minnow. The length between the jig hook and treble hook should be less than the minnows length.

The changes that you can make to lures are unlimited. Anything from shaving the lip of a deep diver to cutting off hooks. Try to adapt to the situation at hand. Fishing will become easier, more productive and more challenging.

D6   RIVERS; THE FALL RUN
              Over And Out

Ice starts to form around the rivers edge. Soon back-bays and creeks freeze up. Walleyes are very active during this time period. Extreme caution must be taken during the thin ice period. The backwater areas may accumulate three or four inches before the river freezes an inch. I have watched fishermen while they slide their boats over the ice into open water. Personally, I don't

favor the idea. Rather than take a chance, fish the dam areas. There are usually plenty of walleyes to be found, or fish from shore.

When the back-bays freeze over, fish the structures that are close to the river bed. Work the shallow water obstructions. Watch the panfish fishermen. Usually perch, crappies and bluegill are very active at this time of year. The walleyes will be near by. Concentrate along the break, especially the one that leads in from the river channel. But be careful for thin ice.

As far as the actual river itself goes, dam areas and open water can be fished productively. But for most fishermen it's over and out until the ice is firm enough to support fishermen.

SECTION IV

LAKE ERIE:
THE NEW HORIZON

A   THE NEW HORIZON

Three elderly gents decided to spend a few days fishing aboard Capt. Claudie Blaha's charter boat. They were promised action. On the first day, walleyes came fast, with arms aching they asked to fish for smallmouth bass on the second day (figuring fishing would be easier). It didn't take long to fill up on the second day so asked to fish for perch on the third day. Well, finally they told Capt. Claudie Blaha that what they had meant by easier fishing was, "They didn't want to catch that many fish, because it was a lot of work". So the remainder of the time, the gents drifted around enjoying the sun. Can you imagine, catching so many fish that the fatigue would get you?

Lake Erie is a real success story. But it did have problems in the earlier days. Due to high Mercury levels, the commercial fishery was cut in 1970. That and environmental protection laws set the stage for a strong comeback in the walleye populations. It did not stop there. The work of fisheries biologists and nature brought the lake to its current condition which is quite clean, producing more fish than ever before and the making of the success story.

Nature has lent a helping hand with higher water levels and some very successful spawning years. Almost every second or third year since 1970 has been great, particularly 1977. The 1977 hatch produced a population explosion that resulted in unbelievable catches of fifteen to twenty two inch fish during the 1979 season. The 1980 season should show fantastic catches of three to five pound fish and 1982 is slated as the trophy walleye fishing year by fisheries biologist Carl Baker. During the 1979 season, there was a ten fish limit. It has been cut to a six fish limit recently. This along with nature's cooperation, should result in many trophy walleye catches during the 1982 season.

Back in the fifties, commercial fishermen caught millions of pounds of walleye. In 1955, the harvest was approximately fifteen million pounds, then it dwindled down to Ohio's 1970 catch of ten thousand pounds. The taking of brood stock and environmental conditions were responsible for the dwindling populations. Canada and other states bordering Lake Erie still have the commercial fisheries. However, Ohio does not, and walleye populations have exploded in the western basin.

The higher water levels have helped to dilute pollutants, thus a new horizon on an old body of water. To continue with the fisheries that Lake Erie now experiences, the DNR must have public support. Support in programs and adhering to recommendations set by the Department of Natural Resources. Carl Baker, a Lake Erie Fisheries Unit

CAPTAIN BART BLAHA, a well-known Lake Erie charter skipper, with a wall-hanger of a walleye.

Program Supervisor at Sandusky Bay has been extremely helpful in providing information for this section. Carl has done a great job and deserves recognition for his knowledgeable input and work done on Lake Erie.

While researching Lake Erie, I did run into something that really bothered me. Commercial fishermen still earn a living with catches of other species of fish, and that's fine and dandy . . . but there is a problem that should be looked into. The size of gill nets used to catch other species also catch plenty of walleyes. The problem is, although the walleyes are thrown back into the lake, in most cases they are dead. Permitting the commercial fishermen to keep only the dead fish would be a problem of regulation.

There is one other possibility: Requiring commercial fishermen to take dead walleyes to a Government station. The cost alone would encourage a commercial fisherman to handle the walleye with care and to use better nets. The government station could process and sell the walleye thereby receiving funds to pour back into programs that are needed on the lake from which the walleye came. Any fisherman that takes away from his natural resources should be concerned enough to give something back to it. This program makes more sense than throwing dead fish back.

CHARTER BOATS drift for walleyes, frequently taking fish just under the surface despite depths of 20 feet or more.

The economic impact from the improved fisheries at Lake Erie has done wonders for many communities. Some of the growth rates and increased business volume has risen thirty to fifty percent in the last couple of years. At times, during the summer, there are lines two miles long at boat launching sites. Plus many farmers have turned vacant fields into parking and launching areas.

Will it last? No one really knows. But if high water trends remain; the environment is protected, common sense regulation enforced and mother nature cooperates Lake Erie could continue to be the most productive walleye lake in the world for sport fishing.

B   THE CHARTER BOAT SCENE

A few years back there were approximately fifteen charter boats operating along the southern shores of the Ohio border. In 1979 that figure rose to over one hundred and fifty. Charter Boat President Capt. Bart Blaha has been a resident in the area since 1960. Bart feels that chartering is the best way for an angler to get the feel for Lake Erie. Besides, it is the safest way to work "big water". Lake Erie can turn from pussy-cat to tiger in a matter of minutes. The charter boat captains don't take chances, safety means a lot more than a dollar to them.

The going rate is between one hundred and eighty dollars and two hundred and fifty dollars per boat load of people. It might sound like a lot but most of the boats have capabilities of holding ten to thirty people comfortably. And for the action that is provided, you can hardly go wrong. Call at least three months ahead of time for a booking. The charters also fish for smallmouth bass (when they are really hot) and perch. Smallmouth bass fishing is highly underrated. The average fish is about two pounds. Capt. Blaha lives in Marblehead, Ohio and can help out with available charters in the association.

C   THE SMALL BOAT AND LAKE ERIE

Small aluminum boats can be used on Lake Erie. Carl Baker suggests at least a seventeen foot boat.

However, many boat rentals have sixteen foot models available. You are not dealing with a small body of water. Currents and storms can create hazardous conditions almost instantly. Most of the small craft boatsmen stay near shore in the western basin where excellent walleye action can be had. An extra kicker motor is adviseable. Also, a distress flare should be on board and C.B. or marine radio if possible.

Some of the islands have regular ferry routes that can transport vehicles and boats. Some of the anglers ferry out to an island and launch. The island areas provide some shelter from the wind. A couple have airports and lodging.

The advantages that small boats have is they can employ a greater number of fishing methods. Could you imagine a charter trying to troll with ten or more people aboard? While chartering, the chief method of fishing is by drifting (which is

STRINGERS OF BIG WALLEYES such as this have made Lake Erie the world's hottest hotspot.

very productive). With a small craft, the fisherman can troll to locate fish quickly and then drift if he so chooses.

The methods of trolling, back-trolling and drifting as discussed in Section II, E6 apply to Lake Erie also. Most of the island areas have decent structure to fish, plus there are many reefs. Some of the reef areas are quite shallow and caution should be taken.

Prior to actually launching, it is wise to get the latest weather information. Also check with local sport shops and marinas as to where the walleyes have been biting. Don't take any unnecessary chances. Most of the boat rentals have restrictions about running their small boats out to the islands.

D FISH MOVEMENT IN THE WESTERN BASIN

Through the help of tagging studies, fishermen and fishery biologists, the general seasonal movements of the walleye are somewhat predictable. Lake Erie has also provided documentary proof of catching suspended walleye on a predictable and consistent basis . . . documentation that will undoubtedly open doors on many inland lakes.

Walleyes spawn in both the Maumee and Sandusky River systems, and later on the reefs located throughout the western basin. Movement into the river systems takes place in February, March and April. Spawning usually occurs during late March and early April. With colder water on the lake, spawning usually takes place during mid-April on the reefs. Walleye movement is controlled by two factors: early in the year, water temperatures; and later, the forage fish movements.

There are two distinct migrational patterns. Generally fish tagged in the Maumee River head north to the Detroit River, while others head easterly towards the islands then north toward deeper water as the summer progresses. Walleyes that spawn in the Sandusky River tend to have some westerly movement; some northerly movement to the island areas; and some easterly movement into the Central portion of Lake Erie. The migrational trend is to head toward the reefs, swinging to the islands, West Sister, South Bass, Middle Bass, North Bass, Big Chicken, then over towards Pelee Island (during fall most of the bigger walleyes came from the west side of Pelee Island) then towards the deeper water just northwest of Pelee. This progression starts just after spawning and slowly moves through its pattern until fall. The best fishing occurs during June and July. Maximum depth in the western basin is approximately thirty-five feet.

Movement of walleye is regulated by the move-ments of its forage. The forage consists of lake shiners, gizzard shad, sheepshead, spottail shiners, white bass, perch, smelt, and alewife. Some are suspended and move laterally, while others are primary bottom feeders. This causes a split in the walleye population. Some of the walleye follow the bottom feeders and others follow to the suspended forage. One very interesting study conducted by Ohio's Department of Natural Resources proves that a split in the walleye population does occur.

In October of 1979, a series of nets were set in different areas of the western basin. In each area, a Kegged net and bottom net (gillnets) were set. The Kegged net is a gill net that is suspended approximately four feet below the surface and extends down seven feet. The nets are 1,300 feet long. The bottom gill net is the same, except that it is on the bottom. The greatest number of walleyes were netted with the Kegged nets. 754 walleyes were caught suspended just under the surface while another 505 walleyes were caught in bottom nets (approximately 20 to 30 feet deep). In each area, walleyes were caught in both surface and bottom nets at the same time. Interestingly enough, in the Middle Sister Island area walleyes were netted two to one in a suspended net; and near the Kelly Island area there were ten suspended walleye to every one caught in bottom nets. The split also showed that each year class was represented in both Kegged and bottom nets. What does it mean? It means that fishermen should be catching suspended walleye on a consistent basis and that the walleye is following its food source. It means that a split actually does occur, that there is documented proof of it, and the possibility of it happening on other lakes that has a substantial suspended forage fish population is very likely. On Lake Erie, fishermen do catch suspended walleyes consistently!

The central and eastern portions of Lake Erie are much deeper and lack the abundance of reefs and island areas. Walleyes that are caught by sport fishermen are generally caught within three miles of shore. There are rock flats that outline the perimeter of Lake Erie. These areas harbor concentrations of walleye during the summer months. In some areas the bottom content changes to sand. The best fishing occurs in the western basin because of the heavy concentration of walleyes within a smaller portion of the lake. There is more structure, and heavier concentrations of baitfish. Besides, fish management has stopped the commercial fishery for walleyes and helped to bring on the walleye boom.

E   HOW TO FISH ON LAKE ERIE

The methods employed are dependent upon your means of transportation. A privately owned boat

offers versatility, as where a charter boat straps the fisherman down to fishing one method. The location is also important. In the western basin, walleyes are so highly concentrated in a relatively small area that drift fishing works. Meanwhile, in the central and eastern portions, walleyes are spread out more and trolling saves time while locating fish (especially when fishing is tough).

All of the trolling methods covered by various chapters in this book work on all lakes, including Lake Erie. But, the time of year is important when selecting depth, because trolling at the correct depth is essential. During spring, trolling is productive in shallow water. Shallow water at this time

A COMMONPLACE CATCH of walleyes in the western basin of Lake Erie. Although Canada and the states bordering Lake Erie still have the commercial fisheries, Ohio does not.

ILLUSTRATION 233

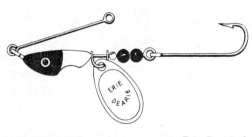

THE ERIE DEARIE, manufactured by Erie Dearie Lure, 2233 Greenville Rd., N.E., Cortland, Ohio 44410.

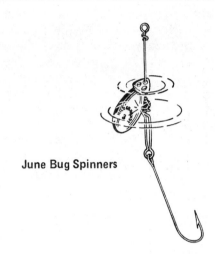

June Bug Spinners

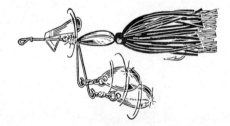

Double Eagle Lure

Naked Nugget

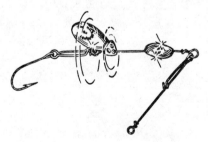

Walleye Whizzo

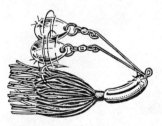

Nugget Lure

Five Hildebrandt lures for Lake Erie walleyes. For best results, it's best to remove the skirts shown on the Nugget and Double Eagle lures. For further information, write: John J. Hildebrandt Corp., P.O. Box 50, Logansport, IN 46947.

means from the surface to approximately twelve feet. When trolling in shallow water, you must let out a substantial amount of line. Walleyes can spook very easily. A long line will help in contacting fish that have spooked briefly. During the early part of summer, the walleyes move out to deeper water, and some to a suspended state. Trolling with bottom bumping lures in approximately twelve feet of water will take some fish. When trolling for suspended fish, work the ten foot level. Troll slowly. Again, a long line will be needed when trolling for the suspended fish; a short almost vertical line when trolling on the bottom. When fish contact is made, throw out a marker buoy. Then work the area thoroughly.

As the summer progresses into late July and August, the split is more pronounced. Some of the walleyes will feed right at the surface even though the lake depth is 30 feet or more. The walleyes are feeding on lake shiners, spot-tail shiners, shad and white bass. At the same time bottom feeding walleyes are relating to perch and sheepshead. In essence, an angler can fish for either the suspended top water walleyes or bottom bump for the deep water fish. If one group is not very active, the fisherman can change lures and work for the other group.

During early fall, the walleyes move onto the shallow reefs again. Others move towards the river systems and some suspend. This is a very brief period lasting approximately a week. Some very large fish are caught during this time. The Pelee Island area (on the west side) has been very productive for the larger fish. As September ends, walleyes tend to move to deeper waters again. Depending on the weather, this period may last several weeks or just a few days. A quick cold spell could bring them back early. During October, walleyes are usually scattered at different depths (which makes fishing tough); and finally as ice forms, walleyes again move to the shallow waters. This is generally during late November or early December.

Trolling at the proper depths, at the correct speed and with the right choice of baits produces fish. Finding the productive combination is what its all about. Like all lakes, Lake Erie has its pet lures. The ones that are used regularly because

they have been productive. The pet lures should be tried first, however, your mind should not close out other possibilities.

The most productive baits (Illustration 233) on Lake Erie are: The Erie Dearie, Hilde's Naked Nugget, The Nugget, Hilde's Double Eagle, The Walleye Whizzo, June Bug Spinner and Reef Runner. For trollers, some of the crankbaits are producing fish. They are usually deep divers. Some smaller lures are trolled deep with Gapen's Bait-Walker. Covering the correct depth is essential.

Troll slowly with a tight-action crankbait. Cover different depths at one hour intervals over structure that is known to harbor walleyes. Most of the forage species are silver in color in open water. In reef areas some are a bit more golden in color.

Baits like the Erie Dearie and Nugget are used with a piece of nightcrawler. The theory is: the piece of nightcrawler emits oils into the water (a walleye can smell its prey). There must be something to it, because side by side the angler using a full crawler catches fewer fish than the one using a piece of crawler on Lake Erie. Cutting off the end piece of a nightcrawler may be worthwhile trying on other lakes too. The piece of crawler is pushed onto the hook and cast or trolled slowly. Depth control with the Erie Dearie and Nugget is achieved by the speed of the troll or retrieve.

Color preferences seem to change both seasonally and daily. Seasonally, in 1978, silver was the hot color; in 1979 both silver and gold were hot with a mild come on with chartruese. Daily switching back and forth from silver to gold. Other colors that have been successful include: yellow, red and white combinations, chartruese, and hot orange.

Other lures that should work (because they are of the same type) include: Twister's Sassy Shad w/spinner, the Beetle Spin, regular spinner baits (hair-pin types), straight line spinners like the Mepps, etc. In crankbaits, try: the Rapala, Sparkle-Tail, Mirror-Lure, Bagley, Bill Norman Baits, Cordell, and Crankbait Corporation Lures.

Troll slowly during spring and fall; and moderately during summer. When using tight-action crankbaits, troll slowly. During spring troll in shallow water; during early summer troll in both deep water and about ten feet down; during summer troll at the surface and in deep water; during early fall troll shallow; during mid-fall troll both deep and shallow (just under the surface over deep water); and during late fall . . . troll shallow.

DRIFTING

On a charter boat, the method most often used is drifting. That's drifting and casting. Ninety percent of the time, the fishermen use baits like the Erie Dearie and Nugget. A piece of nightcrawler is strung on the hook and the casting begins. Usually the captain informs the angler as to what depth count to use. He may instruct two fishermen to use an eight count; two others a ten count and so on. As soon as fish contact is made, the rest of the fishermen use that particular depth count. Here's how it works: in *Illustration 234, Fig. A* fishermen (1) and (2) work the eight count; fishermen (3) and (4) work the ten count and fishermen (5) and (6) work the twelve count (the counts could be less or more depending on time of day and season). Fishermen (1) and (2) cast out; as soon as the bait hits the water, they count, 1001, 1002, etc. up to 1008. The retrieve varies. They might crank seven or eight times, swat the rod tip toward another direction, crank seven or eight times and swat it back . . . doing this all the way back to the boat. At first the speed of retrieve might be slow, then is increased after a number of casts. At times the walleyes want it slow and other times fast, so you must experiment. The other anglers do the same thing at their perspective depths until fish contact is made. In Fig. (B) fish contact was established at the count of twelve. At this point, the other fishermen would switch over to the count of twelve. This is the method used to catch suspended walleyes on Lake Erie. This is done all through the season, but more so during July and August. During June, the walleyes are closer to reefs and the shallow water is worked a majority of the time.

With the vast expansions of water, you are probably wondering, Where does a fisherman start? Obviously, the western basin of Lake Erie is unique because of the astronomical number of walleyes present. Plus, communication between charter boats helps to cut down the odds. However, the fact remains, that a substantial number of walleyes do suspend and feed quite heavily. Something that happens on lakes that have a heavy suspended forage fish population. It is not a freak event that only happens on Lake Erie.

There are a few ways that can cut down on the amount of water that is to be explored for suspended walleye. As the summer progresses, the general (even though suspended near the surface) trend is to move towards deeper waters. So this in itself cuts down on the area. Secondly, they seem to take up in areas that are coined "loafing areas" by Carl Baker, or milling areas. There must be a substantial suspended forage fish population, residing in the loafing area. In *Illustration 235*, walleyes move toward the deeper water. In this particular case, resident reef and island walleyes move toward the same deep water area. These fish feed on the suspended baitfish populations in the loafing area. Some will be bottom feeders while the majority will feed on the suspended forage.

Another way to locate the suspended walleye is by using your depth finder or graph. Schools of baitfish will show up as small marks on the graph or a series of light blips on the depth finder. It is generally accepted that the walleyes will be slightly under the baitfish, except when feeding, then they will be mixed right in with the baitfish. Learning to interpret the depth finder will help in locating fish. A good choice in graphs is the Lowrance 1510, 515A, or 1510B. In depth finders; Lowrance's 360, LFD-1240 and LFG-1230, Hummingbird Super Sixty and shallow water thirty.

Lake Erie fishermen have found heavy schools of walleye under schools of white bass. The problem has been to present a bait to these walleyes because the white bass seem to hit almost anything. And to find white bass and walleyes, watch the birds. The birds are usually diving and feeding on minnows that white bass and walleye kick up to the surface. Charter boat captains are on the constant lookout for feeding birds.

When locating a school of fish, most of the fish are of the same age group; small fish with small fish and larger fish with large fish. This is not to say that the rule is rigid, it is a generality.

ILLUSTRATION 234

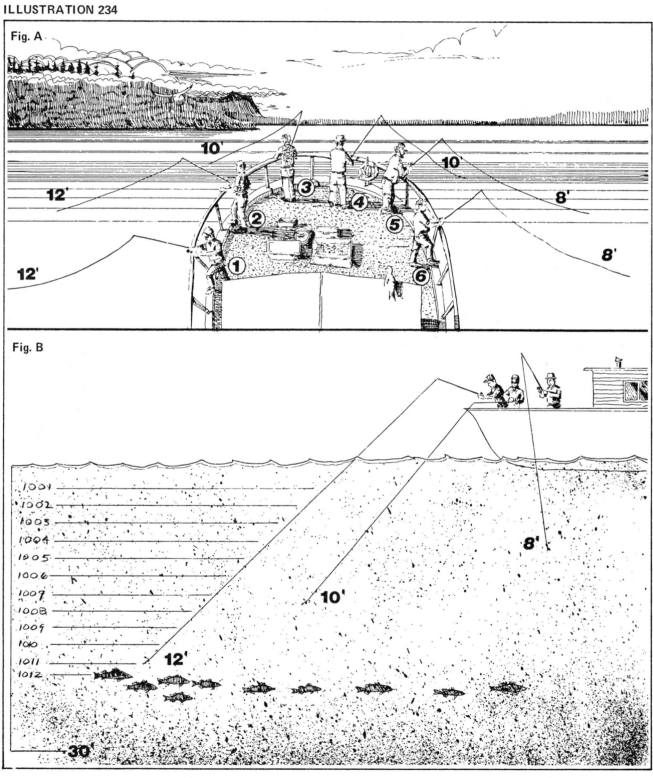

Fig. A

Fig. B

ILLUSTRATION 235

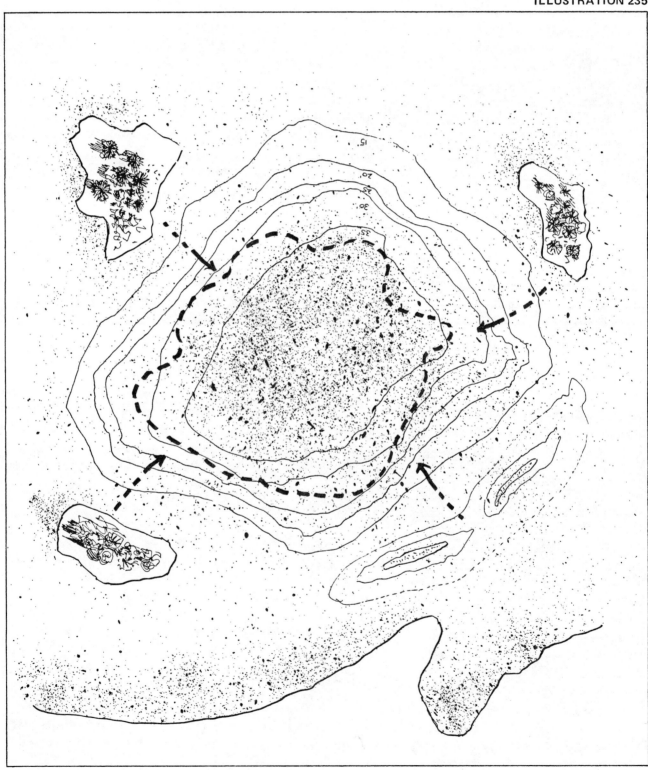

F   APPLYING LAKE ERIE METHODS
        TO OTHER LAKES

Lake Erie should be looked at as a learning center. It's unique because there's an astronomical number of walleyes and heavy fishing pressure (although the fishing mortality rate among walleyes is less than thirty-five percent). Much can be learned from the exhilarated fishing pressure in the western basin of Lake Erie. Fishermen will stumble on to new fishing methods at a quicker pace. Capt. Blaha said, "Ten years ago, you never heard of anyone catching suspended walleyes on Lake Erie, but now it is the most productive way fish!" As time progressed, charter boats followed migrations of suspended walleyes and found productive methods of catching them. Before this, the walleyes seemed to disappear, just as they seem to disappear on other lakes that have suspended forage. Before the awakening, *Lake Erie fishermen experienced the same frustration that many fishermen feel right now on lakes that have suspended forage.*

How different is Lake Erie? It has substantial suspended fish populations . . . but so do many of our deep bodies of water. There is little difference in the environment . . . and the walleye does not know whether it's in Lake Erie, Lake Geneva, Lake Mille Lacs, Lake Winnebago, Geers Ferry Reservoir, etc. It only knows that the laws of survival are clear cut. It must stay in proximity to its food. The biggest difference between Lake Erie and most of the other bodies of water is the number of walleye per acre. Some of the suspended walleye schools are a mile long and half mile wide. Relating to other lakes, it means searching for smaller schools of suspended walleye. That can be accomplished by trolling.

Try the Lake Erie methods on lakes that are near your home. Make sure that the lake has an abundant population of both walleye and suspended forage fish. It's a new dimension of fishing that hasn't been explored on other lakes.

SECTION V
WALLEYE FISHING TOOLS

A1 THE ROD
Back-Trolling Rod

Back-trolling does not necessarily require a specialty rod. However, if back-trolling is a method that you use often, then a special spinning rod should be purchased. A relatively stiff (but not muskie stiff) rod is required to have continuous sensitive feeling. The back-trolling rod allows you to feel messages transmitted through the line and rod. For this a five and one half to six foot heavy action graphite rod is needed. There have been times that I produced fish because I felt the hit while other anglers using the same biat in the same boat failed to feel a light hit with their fiberglass rods. Setting the hook immediately is important. The graphite rod does not have tremor, therefore, a split second is saved when setting the hook. It helps to make you a bit quicker on the draw. The shaft of the back-trolling rod is thin with stiff action all the way through to the tip.

Some of the best on the market include: Skyline's 6007, Lamiglas 1216 and Lake King's SG-3. A long cork handle and fixed reel seat is preferred over a cork handle with sliding ring because strength in the butt section is essential.

A back-trolling rod and jigging rod are very close in action, because of the strength that is needed to drive those hooks home. The five and one half to six foot lengths are desired. The longer the rod, the lesser the strength in setting the hook.

A2 NIGHTCRAWLER ROD

A specialty nightcrawler rod is six and one half to seven and one half feet long, has a long cork handle, and is relatively stiff. A medium heavy action will suffice. A salmon-egg rod often times fills-the-bill. The spinning rod is long and stiff, which allows long smooth casts with little effort. With this setup you can cast effortlessly with a very small split-shot and nightcrawler, without losing the nightcrawler. Both Fenwick and Diawa manufacture fiberglass rods of this type. In graphite which is a preferred material because of its ability to have length and strength, Lamiglas and Lake King offer excellent rods.

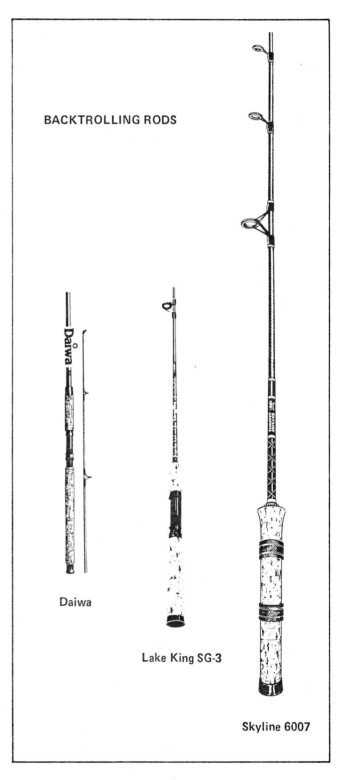

BACKTROLLING RODS

Daiwa

Lake King SG-3

Skyline 6007

A3   JIGGING ROD

Jig fishermen are very demanding when it comes to the type of rod used. Often times they must snap a jig through the weeds, plus feel messages transmitted through the line. In essence the rod must be strong, sensitive and have aluminum oxide guides to prevent wear and tear on the line. To save money, the jigging and back-trolling rod could be the same rod.

Graphite rods are very strong and sensitive. Some are getting down into the working mans' price range. Pflueger's G359, five foot nine inch rod is inexpensive and a good choice for jigging. Other excellent graphite spinning rods for jigging include: Skyline's 607 and 6007, Lake King's SG-3, and the Lamiglas 1216.

Here is an experiment that will convince you of the difference in sensitivity between graphite and fiberglass. Take two rods of the same length and action, one of each material. Tie a piece of twelve pound test monofilament to each tip top guide. Trim the ends down to about four inches. Now hold the rod and ask someone to just barely touch the piece of monofilament. You will feel the slightest touch on the graphite rod and hardly nothing on the fiberglass rod. This is the fish catching difference.

A4   ARTIFICIAL BAIT ROD

Specifically, a crankbait rod. The heavy stiff actions used for trolling and jigging are usually not used for casting lures. The artificial bait rod is usually a bait-casting rod, has medium action and is between five and one half and six feet long. Because of constant casting, aluminum oxide guides are required to cut down on line wear. In fiberglass material a medium heavy action is preferred; in graphite material, a medium action. A medium action rod can help to impart action on the lure. The rod should be sensitive enough to feel the obstructions that the lure bumps.

There are many good rods on the market, particularly in this action. Some are: Lake King's CLG 4, CLMG 3, CGS Med.; Skyline's SKC 5508; Fenwick's Lunkerstik 2000; Shimano's GR01553;

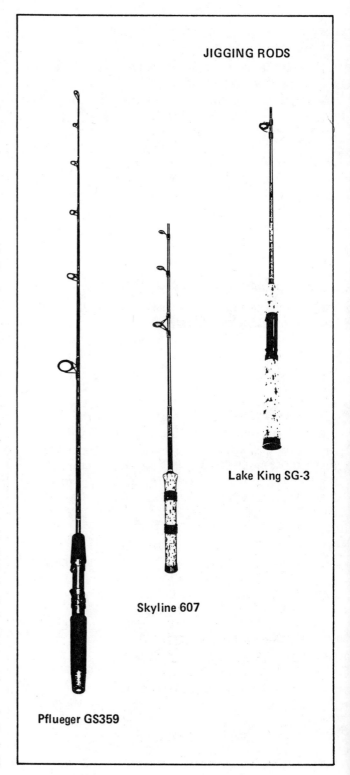

JIGGING RODS

Lake King SG-3

Skyline 607

Pflueger GS359

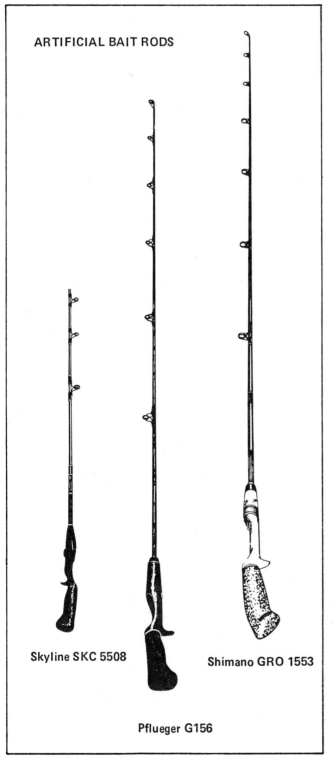

ARTIFICIAL BAIT RODS

Skyline SKC 5508

Shimano GRO 1553

Pflueger G156

Pflueger's G156 and Lew Childre's 1-26H0BB. That ought to be enough to give you an idea of the action.

When fishing shallow in clear lakes, casts are often times long. A rod must help in whipping out the cast while maintaining a smooth effortless release.

B1   THE REEL
Ultra-Light Spinning

Ultra-light spinning is for the light tackle enthusiast. Such equipment is usually used by panfish fishermen. However, more and more walleye fishermen are using it for fishing in clear water lakes. The ultra-light spinning reels are loaded with four or six pound test monofilament line. Occasionally the walleyes are very finicky and light lines help to trick them into striking.

The drag system of the spinning reel is very important. The best reels have a drag system that is separate from the spool release nut. Some of the cheaper reels have a nut that tightens or loosens the drag and when removed, the spool can be taken off. The drag has a tendency to loosen while fishing. The better reels have a button that is pushed into release the spool. The drag remains set. The reels cost more but they are worth it.

There are many fine ultra-light spinning reels on the market. Some of the better ones are: Zebco's Cardinal 3; Garcia's 308A, 408, 908, and 3800; Daiwa's GS-10 and 10X; and Penn 722Z.

Many of the spinning reels have skirted spools now. This prevents the line from wrapping around the shaft behind the spool. There are both external and internal trips. The internal trips are smoother. However, there is not enough difference to sway your decision. Just make sure that the reel has a good reliable drag system that doesn't stick.

B2   MEDIUM SPINNING

Medium spinning reels are the most popular for walleye fishing. The reel should have a line capacity of two hundred yards of eight pound monofilament line or more. You will never really have occasion to use that much line and probably put a hundred yards of backing on, anyway. But long line trolling requires more line so the capacity should be there. Big bulky spinning reels aren't needed for walleye fishing.

The drag system is important. The push button release spool is best. But having the drag system in back of the reel like the Cardinal 4 is excellent also. The drag should not react to weather and should have memory. This means to have the ability to remain at a prescribed setting. Some drags stick; suddenly they let go and you must reset it.

Here are some good choices; Daiwa's GS-13; Garcia's Cardinal 54; the Garcia Mitchell 300A and Garcia 3000; and Penn 714Z. There are other good ones on the market; the list gives you a starting point.

B3   BAIT-CASTING

With the sophistication that comes with modern day bait-casting reels also comes high prices. You just can't afford to make mistakes when purchasing a fifty or sixty dollar reel. Besides the higher price of materials, the cost is reflected by intricate drag and gear systems. The reels are becoming lighter in weight and precision made for easier casting. They are so easy that occasionally a fisherman forgets to thumb the spool upon release, so an occasional "birds nest" evolves. But for the most part, they are so easy to use that one can learn within minutes.

When walleye fishing, most of your bait-casting is done with crankbaits and other lures used for trolling. Innovations in design make bait-casting easy with a minimum amount of backlashes or

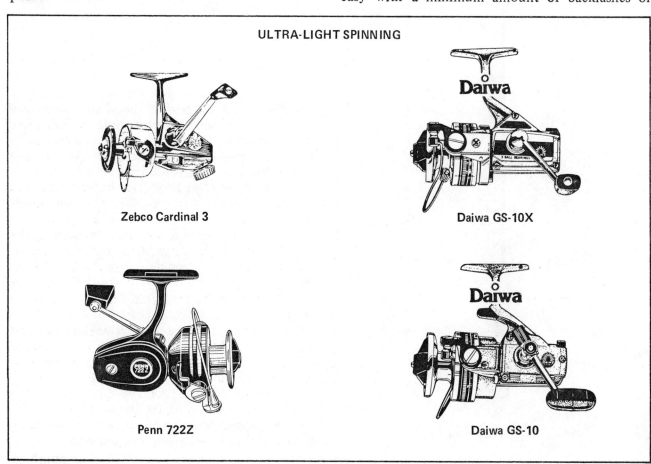

ULTRA-LIGHT SPINNING

Zebco Cardinal 3

Daiwa GS-10X

Penn 722Z

Daiwa GS-10

"bird nests". It is not necessary to have a reel that has the capabilities of holding a large amount of line. Some of the best on the market include Shimano's Bantam 100, 100Ex, and 200. The earlier models had plastic line guides which broke quite easily. The new ones have aluminum guides (the factory has been very good about replacing the plastic guides with aluminum guides); Garcia's 4500C and 4500BC; Penn's Level Matic reels; Quick's Champion 700B and Daiwa's Millionaire Reels are all decent. Shimano offers the smoothest, but it is expensive.

B4   CONVENTIONAL REELS

Conventional reels are of the same basic design as bait-casting reels except they are used for trolling. The well rounded walleye fisherman is going to do

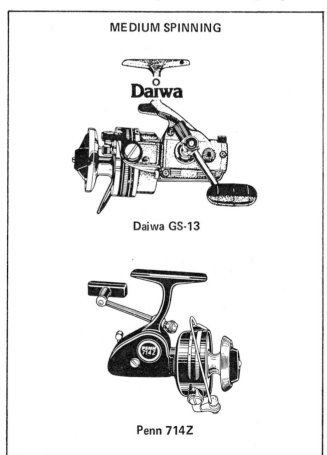

MEDIUM SPINNING

Daiwa GS-13

Penn 714Z

some trolling. If he does a lot of trolling, I recommend trolling with wire line when trolling in deep water. The lure will travel deeper, quicker. It is easier to follow the contour.

The reel should have a line guide, otherwise spooling is uneven. The conventional reels range greatly in price. You can get a decent one for twenty to thirty dollars. The reel should have a good drag system, and be capable of holding more than two hundred yards of fifteen pound test line. When trolling with wire line, use fifteen to twenty-five pound test.

There are several fine conventional reels on the market. Some of the better ones include: Penn Peer 109 MF, 209 MF (for the proper amount of wire line capacity); and Shakespeare 1950. A regular bait-casting reel can be used, however, having a reel specifically setup for trolling eliminates a lot of wasted time.

C1   THE BOAT
The Trolling And Back-Trolling Rig

The type of boat needed will be determined by the size of lake most often fished and number of people you fish with. A trolling rig for Lake Erie would hardly be suitable for a small shallow body of water. Besides, boat control is essential, and those big rigs just don't have it.

Successful forward trolling is based on a good marriage between boat and motor. An unbalanced rig can be tough to troll from. Outboard motors can be trolled down to a crawl when in the one and one half to thirty-five horse power range, plus Mercury's fifty horsepower outboard with its four cyclinders can also troll down to a crawl. An outboard with a tiller handle offers the greatest amount of control.

The rig itself can be aluminum or fiberglass and in the fourteen to seventeen foot range. Smaller boats limit you to the type of water that can be safely fished; and larger boats need more horses, so control is sacrificed. Forward and back-trolling can be accomplished with the same rig.

Back-trolling is a method that offers total boat control. The motor acts as a pivot point allowing you to cover structure accurately. The outboard

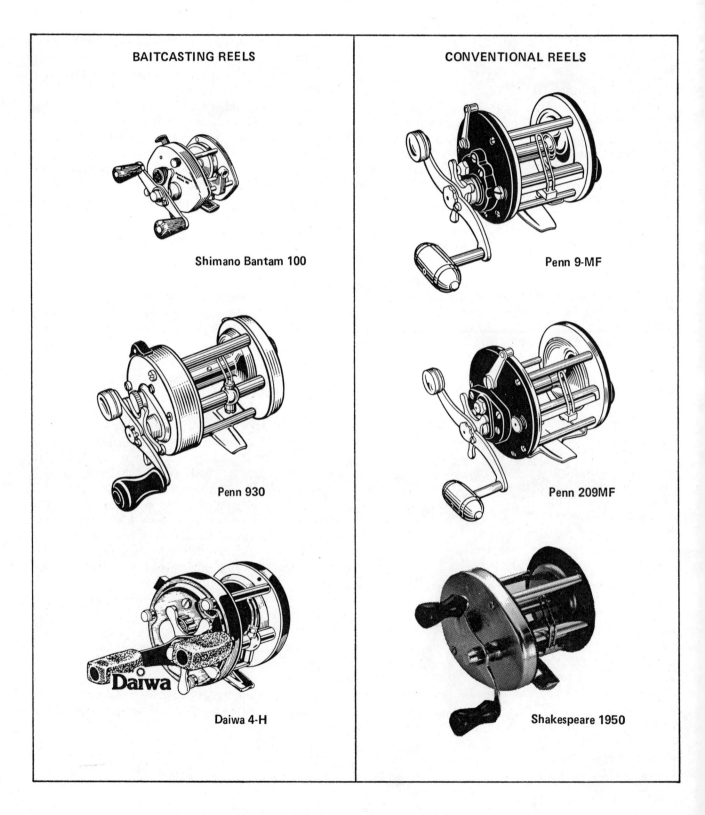

BAITCASTING REELS

CONVENTIONAL REELS

Shimano Bantam 100

Penn 9-MF

Penn 930

Penn 209MF

Daiwa 4-H

Shakespeare 1950

motor must be working properly and have the capabilities to maintain crawling trolling speeds. The best rig and motor combinations that I have found is; a Tuffy Roustabout (Mfg. by Glasway, Inc., Lake Mills, Wisconsin), with a twenty-five horse-power Johnson or Evinrude; a Lund Pike Boat with a twenty to thirty-five horse-power motor; and Ranger's 1600V with a fifty horse-power Mercury. Other boats having the approximate weight (without console) and matched up with an outboard of thirty horse-power and less (with the exception of the four cyclinder Mercury fifty horse-power engine which really trolls down well), with a twenty inch or higher transom can be considered also.

The back-trolling coterie of fishermen usually have their boats setup for that type of fishing. Splash guards are used to keep the water from splashing over the transom when trolling against the waves on a windy day. You can purchase a set of splash guards for under sixty dollars (Glasway, Inc., 865 East Stony Road, Lake Mills, Wisc. 53551) or make your own from truck splash guards. The installation is quite easy. Fishermen remove them at times, so a holding bracket is installed. The splash guards slide into the bracket. The inside rubber ridge is cut to form around the motor. Occasionally a fisherman will want his electric motor on the transom. To accomplish this, cut another slot into the splash guard. Make it long enough for the shaft of the electric motor. Now with electric motor in place, secure a piece of rubber around the shaft but attached to the splash guard. This cuts down on the amount of water that might come over the transom at the electric motor opening.

The boat should have an adaquate bilge pump. Common sense should be used. I know of some fishermen that back-troll in three and four foot waves. You are just asking for trouble when taking those kinds of chances.

On a real calm day, use the electric motor to back-troll. On windy days use the outboard, and on moderately rough water . . . troll forward or drift. Most back-trollers have their electric motors attached to the transom. Depth finders and tackle are located near the back of the boat. They set up

their rigs so there is a minimum of body movement while fishing. Shift handle kits can be purchased for the Evinrude and Johnson motors. They are really handy. The shift handle kit allows the fisherman freedom of one hand. The kit includes an extended handle; a push button for shifting changes and throttle, all in the handle. You don't have to reach around the motor to change gears. Usually the back-troller is constantly shifting from reverse to neutral and visa-versa.

C2   THE BOAT
The Positioning Rig

When a fisherman thinks of a positioning rig, the bass boat comes to mind. Electric motors are placed on the bow along the locator and pedestal seat. The fisherman that already has a bass boat has practically eliminated himself from back-trol-

SPLASH GUARDS are used when back-trolling to keep water from splashing over the transom. They're a necessity when trying to hold tight to structure on windy days.

ling. However, the rig can be used for positioning while walleye fishing, just as he would for bass fishing.

Positioning along breaks, points and weeds as discussed throughout this book can be productive when walleye fishing. If you continue to fish smaller waters I suggest that you purchase a rig that is practical for this type of fishing.

Trolling backwards for accuracy will not work with the larger boats. Most outboards have through the hub exhaust systems. The backup of water can mess up your motor. Besides, trolling backwards with a large rig presents problems as far as accuracy is concerned. Forward trolling with the larger motors, gets them carboned up quickly and at times causes over-heating. It almost forces the fisherman to troll faster than he might want to.

When purchasing an electric motor for a heavy boat, find one that has enough thrust. Enough to hold you in a strong wind and low enough to just barely crawl along on calm days. In the twelve-twenty-four volt system, electric motors with thirty or more pounds of thrust are available, they are variable and can get down to approximately eight or ten pounds of thrust. That's enough thrust to move a large boat around.

C3 THE BOAT
A Little Of Both Worlds

The all around fisherman should purchase a rig that will; first, fulfill his needs when fishing for his most-sought-after species; and secondly, be flexible enough to be able to fish for other species as well. Often times it is difficult to find a rig that will be suitable for both worlds.

The boat should have plenty of room for muskie and northern pike fishing. Have back-trolling capabilities with a high transom, relatively light weight (under seven or eight hundred pounds). Have a deck for bass fishing. A flat floor for both comfort and stability and handle both the smallest and larger lakes. Finding that kind of rig is difficult indeed.

I have found three rigs that fill-the-bill. My first choice is manufactured by Glasway, Inc., it is the Tuffy Marauder. It has all of the mentioned ca-

pabilities (other smaller models are available, and are excellent choices for waters that you can see across). The Tuffy Marauder is sixteen feet, six inches long, has a twenty and one half inch transom height and is rated for a fifty horse-power motor. I recommend a thirty-five horse-power motor. My second choice is the Ranger 1600V. However, a fifty horse-power Mercury does a better job than lower horse-power engines on this rig. And for large bodies of water the Lund Pike 16D or eighteen footer does an excellent job. The Pike 16-D should be matched with a thirty-five Johnson or Evinrude and the Pike 18 should be used with a fifty-horse-power Mercury.

My choices are based upon practical use. You may have other choices, just make sure that the rig will do the job for you. As time goes on, you may change your specific preference. Be prepared for it, it will save you dollars in the long run.

D1 COLD WATER FISHING ATTIRE
TIPS FOR ICE-FISHING ATTIRE

Insulated underwear, a wool shirt and a snowmobile suit are great for ice fishing or other cold weather activity. However, wearing all of these items at the same time can create difficulties. Sweating from the inside is worse than a slight chill from the outside. If thermo underwear is worn with a wool shirt and heavy pants plus a medium weight jacket . . . that should be quite warm. Plus packing a blanket or wind shield for protection when sitting on a bucket should do the job. While walking out to a prospective ice fishing spot leave your jacket slightly open unless the weather is too bad. This helps to keep you from sweating. Heavy sweating leaves you with an uncomfortable wet feeling and can lead to the chills and possible illness.

If wearing a snowmobile suit, wear long thick socks, heavy pants and shirt. I will usually take my jacket off when drilling holes. I personally like the two piece suit. If the weather turns warm, I will remove the jacket and keep the warm bottoms on.

There are several snowmobile suit manufacturers. Most manufacture both the single and double piece suits. A snowmobile suit should be light enough

THE BOAT

Tuffy Marauder

Ranger 1600 V

(in weight) to wear all day without fatigue, warm enough to with stand extremely cold temperatures, and trap air helping to keep body moisture at a minimum. Some of the better ones that I have found are The Coldmaster Down Coat and Down High-Bib Pants. The Coldmaster is filled with Hanso Branta Prime Northern Silver-Grey™ Goose Down. It has many pockets including hand-warmer pockets. It is light weight and comfortable for wearing all day. Another great outfit is manufactured by Stearns Manufacturing Co. It's call the Brrr Suit. The suits are available in both the single and double piece styles. The Brrr Suit has a durable nylon shell that keeps out cold air and water. Like the Coldmaster, zippers extend down the legs and double-zipper in the jacket. These snowmobile suits are of the highest quality and will give you years of good service.

Wear a pair of heavily insulated boots. Besides the heavy socks, try taking bread wrappers and slide them over the socks. Use a rubber band to hold them up. Then slide the boots on. This keeps your feet dry and helps retain body warmth.

D2   ACCESSORIES

A face mask, or thermal knit face mask helps to prevent wind burn. Pull the face mask down when walking and sitting during windy days. Keep at least three pair of gloves in plastic bags in your sled or bucket.

Take a Catalytic heater along (between two thousand and five thousand BTU unit is enough) to help keep warm. Place it on the upwind side to offset the cold air.

A hand warmer will help to keep your hands warm, and when placed in a pocket helps to keep your body warm. Hand warmers are inexpensive and easy to use. The best ones are just under ten dollars.

A turtle neck sweater keeps the cold out by helping to retain body heat. If your neck is bothered by turle necks, wear a scarf.

The bright reflection of snow really hurts the eyes, even though the day may be cloudy. The affect is so blinding that frequently it takes a minute or two to adjust when entering the house or building. A pair of sunglasses protects the eyes from wind and bright snow.

A weather-shield hot-seat (in blaze orange) is used for seating. The comfortable cushion doesn't use any fuels, chemicals, or electricity. It radiates heat when touched or sat upon. The Super Hot-Seat can be carried on your belt by the clip that is provided. It is a very light weight cushion. All of the accessories can make your day a more comfortable one.

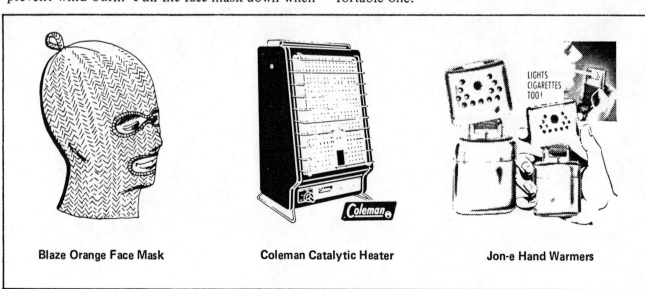

Blaze Orange Face Mask   Coleman Catalytic Heater   Jon-e Hand Warmers

STORIES OF THE OLD DUCK HUNTERS & OTHER DRIVEL
Gordon MacQuarrie

Nineteen of the beloved, best remembered outdoor stories by one of the greatest outdoor writers of all time. *"His interpretations of the outdoors, told with unforgettable zest and humor, went far beyond humor to come to grips with life; what to get out of it and what it means."* — *ZACK TAYLOR*

$5.95 *(Softbound)*

SECRETS OF A MUSKIE GUIDE
Tony Rizzo

A complete tactical guide based on muskie behavior according to seasonal water temperatures. *"Unlike many books which purport to reveal 'secrets' but merely rehash old material, this book contains exactly what its title suggests."* — *SPORTS AFIELD*

$6.00 *(Softbound)*

BIRD HUNTING TACTICS
David Michael Duffey

An extremely practical book written for hunters by a hunter without pretense. If you hunt and admire ruffed grouse; woodcock; pheasants; sharptails; quail and hungarian partridge, this is the one book you must have in your library. *"...Delightful reading and covers the subject beautifully. Duffey knows what he's talking about, whether it is the birds, the dogs, the proper guns or the techniques."* — *FRANK WOOLNER*

$5.95 *(Softbound)*

EUROPEAN RECIPES FOR AMERICAN FISH & GAME
David Backus

Forty-four hearty yet elegant gourmet recipes for freshwater fish, venison, big game, small game and mouth-watering accompaniments. "A loving celebration of pure products, fairly harvested."

$4.50 *(Softbound)*

THE BUCKS CAMP LOG 1916 - 1928
An American Deer Camp Diary

"These short-tailed bucks are a suspicious lot," wrote the Stump Fire Ranger in 1918 "They think that if this book is not written in every night they will suffer the punishment of poor hunting when they cross the River Jordan." The colorful members of Bucks Camp, a northern Wisconsin deer camp, have long since crossed that river, but they left behind this day-to-day record of their spirited, hilarious and sometimes tragic events. More than a nostalgic hunting diary, there is a spirit, a quality to The Bucks Camp Log that reminds hunters everywhere of the grand traditions and skills, the love of nature and comradeship, passed on for generations, that constitute our great hunting heritage.

$5.95 *(Hardbound)*

MAIL ALL ORDERS (include $1.00 shipping & handling) TO:

WILLOW CREEK PRESS
P.O. BOX 2266 / OSHKOSH, WISCONSIN 54903